THE

Purpose

ROOM

A Meeting Place Where You Discover, Accomplish,
and Birth Your God Given Purpose

Table of Contents

Dedication vi

Thank You: vii

Introduction ix

Chapter 1: Step into the Purpose Room 1

Chapter 2: What are you afraid of? 16

Chapter 3: Crying over spilled milk 33

Chapter 4: Where has God placed you now? 44

Chapter 5: What is your Purpose? 61

Chapter 6: Talent vs. Purpose 75

Chapter 7: Mouth to Heart Connection 83

Chapter 8: Refusing to Compare your Purpose
Pregnancy 92

Chapter 9: The Garden of your Heart 101

Chapter 10: Are You Contaminated? 122

Chapter 11: Birthing your Purpose 129

Dedication

This book is dedicated to my Pinky Promise Sisters. I
pray that you walk in the purpose that the Lord has
given you, and that you never, ever stop. Don't quit,
don't look to the right or to the left. Trust in God's
sweet timing and don't ever, ever think that you
don't have value on this earth. You are born for such
a time as this. Continue in your sisterhood, and
develop accountability. You have no idea how God
will use your godly friends in your purpose. We are
the body of Christ and we MUST stick together! I love
you all so much!

Thank You:

My Jesus: Can I ever thank you enough for dying for me? You have literally taken a broken, messed up girl, and given her purpose when this world threw her away. Thank you for loving me unconditionally. Thank you for dying for me. Thank you for sending the Holy Spirit to help me. Thank you for reconciling me back to Jesus. Words cannot express my thankfulness, so I will prove my love for you with my life. I am Yours forever.

My husband, Cornelius Lindsey: Do you know how much you inspire me, and push me closer to Jesus? You challenge me to walk in my calling like no other. Thank you for your love, your support, your encouragement, and just being there for me. I love you with all of me.

My sweet Logan & Taylor: You both have given me a brand new outlook on life and a new reason to *live*. You have given me purpose on a new and special level. You are truly gifts from the Lord. We prayed for you both, and the Lord heard our cries. Thank you for being my first ministry.

My amazing family: Thank you for always supporting me, loving me, and simply being there for me. I appreciate your help with our babies as we accomplish what the Lord has called us to do.

Juliette Bush: To my assistant that literally helps me all day and night. I can email this girl at 2am and get a happy response. Thank you for being obedient to the Lord, and being so faithful in working with me. God will trust you with so much more because you truly work as unto Him alone!

Dominique Bozeman: Thank you for editing my book, challenging me to explain more, and to dig deeper. You truly have a gift from the Lord. I appreciate you, and I look forward to working with you for my next at least 40 books! ☺

Karolyne Roberts: Thank you for formatting my book. You have such a pure, gentle heart, and I cannot wait for this world to see what the Lord has placed in you!

Introduction

Don't skip this part.

Can I keep it real with you? Of all the books that I have written, the process for this one has been the hardest. I have two small children that keep me pretty busy, while simultaneously managing my home as a wife, and running multiple businesses. As I would literally *fight* to write this book, the Lord revealed to me a valuable lesson: **we no longer have excuses as to why we cannot do what He has purposed us to do.** As I was continuing to put off writing for other obligations, the Lord literally woke me up one morning and said, "Finish this book. It is not about you, but it is for who I want it to reach. This book will not write itself." I was procrastinating on finishing this book because I assumed that I could always finish, "tomorrow."

Procrastination is a prideful fruit of the flesh. Pride says, "I will have *tomorrow* to do it," so you keep putting off the steps the Lord has told you to take. Each day, you say, "Don't worry Lord, *tomorrow* I will do what you told me to do!" *Tomorrow*, I will write the book. *Tomorrow* I will start the non-profit for single mothers. *Tomorrow* I will start the non-profit for women who have been living in human trafficking.

Tomorrow I will apply for the job, Lord! *Tomorrow* I will walk by faith. *Tomorrow*.

How do you even know that you will have tomorrow? How prideful are we to think that we control our days? Our days are not our own. They do not belong to us. Our entire life is in the hands of our Lord, Jesus Christ. So, with urgency, I am telling you that if He is instructing you to do some things, you *have* to do them. You *have* to walk by faith. You *have* to keep putting one foot in front of the other and living for Him. I know you don't understand, I know you don't feel confident in your calling, I know you may be thinking, "Why does today, or this, and that matter?" It matters because God is *using* you for such a time as this, for such a *season* as this, and it's important that you blaze forward, and do what He is telling *you*, yes, *you* to do.

Maybe you don't know where to start, and if that's you, I want you to know that today actually matters for your purpose. You are either making progress towards Jesus, or you are hardening your heart against Him. I am not telling you to run out of the particular season you are in, but I *am* telling you to surrender. Surrender yourself, your current season, your situation, your past, your hurts, your pains and your frustrations to the Lord. We cannot carry our past with us, *unless* we are free from it; only that our struggles may be of use to others. I openly share my past because I am not in bondage to it. I am not the Heather I used to be! The Holy Spirit has done a work in my heart. He has saved me, set me free, delivered me, and literally carries me through each day, and I believe He wants to do the same for you.

You're pregnant sister. You're pregnant *with purpose*. I know you don't feel like it. I know it seems like you don't have a plan for your life. I know you don't understand why some things have happened the way that they have, but when God created the heavens and the earth in Genesis, and even before that moment, He assigned you with purpose and a plan. God was thinking about you when He created all things. Your steps were ordered before that moment. How powerful is that? Jeremiah 1:5 says, "Before I formed you in the womb I knew you, before you were born I set you apart." Simply put, God has a purpose for creating you, and has placed you on this earth to solve a problem, but unfortunately, we are creating more problems because we are out of position.

With tears in my eyes, I am telling you, God has a plan for your life. As the Holy Spirit uses me, I'm here to help you see that God has never forgotten about you. I want you to know that no matter how old you are, God made you, and designed you to accomplish a purpose here on this earth. I know people have told you that you don't have a purpose. I know you have a shy personality, and you're wondering why or how God could use you, but He *longs* to use you. Yes, *you*. I know you are a stay at home mom, super swamped in school, or just plain overworked in general, barely finding time to read this book, but even in being a stay at home mother, **God is using you to plant eternal seeds in your children.** Even as a student, God is using you to reach your peers. As an employee, God has made your job your ministry. Whether you're a college student worried about life after graduation, unemployed, or you're at a job that you're not crazy about, **God still desires to use you right where you are**.

Right in the midst of your insecurities, or feeling like you're not enough; right in the middle of you feeling frustrated and overwhelmed in your life—**your today is your mission field**. It may not seem as glamorous as you imagined, but I want you to know that it's preparing you and developing you for *eternity*.

In this book, as the Lord uses me, I want to be your **Purpose Midwife.** I want to assist you in giving birth to that which God has called you. I want to help you realize that you're so purposed, that you don't have to copy anybody, and that God wants to use you right where you are. You don't have to pursue get-rich-schemes, while filling up your time doing what **God never told you to create.** Many of us are pursuing things on this earth that God never designed for us to chase. My heart's cry is that you stop making excuses, and doubting your God-given ability, in order to truly press forward to find that passion and purpose for which God specifically created *you* for.

Chapter 1:

Step into the

Purpose Room

My name is Heather Lindsey, and welcome to the Purpose Room! This is our place to sit down together, grab some tea, and discuss what is going on in your life. It's a place to discover, accomplish, and birth that purpose that God has placed on the inside of you. I would like to think of myself as your midwife. Not for a physical baby, but for what God has created you to do. I'm going to help you birth your purpose baby.

A midwife takes no credit for the baby in your tummy as the Lord opens up your womb. She simply assists the woman in childbirth, or in our case, **in birthing your purpose**. So, step into your purpose appointment and let's get started. Like any pregnancy, you have check-ups to monitor the growth of your baby; well, I pray that the Lord uses these chapters to do check-ins on your heart to see if you're truly growing in Him, or trusting in your own ability.

By the end of this book, my prayer is that you know without a shadow of a doubt what God has called you to do. When you have an understanding of your purpose, you won't be concerned about what others have to say about you. You won't compare your calling to their calling, or worry about, "When is it my time," because you will be so sure about what God told you to do, that you will actually enjoy the journey. It is often those times where we feel like things are silent that we question God's timing, or His will for us, but when you are constantly communicating with the Lord, you don't give in to these questions. He gives you a peace that surpasses all understanding. He encourages you with the knowledge that He has not forgotten about you. He reminds you that He's right there with you—**You just cannot give up hope**.

I sense that there are many women that feel just because they have a past, the Lord cannot use them. Just because they've had an abortion, the Lord cannot use them. Just because they've married an ungodly man, the Lord cannot use them. This is a lie from the pit of hell. God desires to use you no matter where you are, what you are doing, or who you used to be. The question is, are you letting go of your past, repenting of your sins, and turning to Him? Repenting of your sins means, "To turn in the other direction." **There is a corresponding action to your faith**. It says, "Lord, because you saved me, I'm no longer going to hang out at the club at night, get drunk, sleep around, cheat on my husband, or whatever else." You cannot continue in your past, or current, sin and expect to see your purpose tomorrow.

Would I give my 1-year-old daughter, Taylor, a knife? Of course not, but when she's of age, I will gladly give her a knife to cut her Portobello mushroom sandwich (Hey, hopefully she will remain a vegetarian like her mama! ☺) You see, Taylor's not ready for a knife because she hasn't matured enough to understand its purpose. She could hurt herself, and so can you if you get promoted too quickly, or if you are given your purpose before it's time.

I can recall a time when I struggled greatly with my purpose. The first time I ever heard what God called me to do, I was sitting on my rented bed in a two-bedroom apartment in College Park, Maryland. I was there for an internship, and it was my senior year in college. I had finally broke things off with my little boyfriend, which is what pushed me so far into the arms of the Lord, because that relationship was so dysfunctional. So, I'm sitting in my bedroom on a Friday evening, having a date night with the Lord. As I talked with the Lord about the food, our movie, and my week, He instructed me to turn the television off.

Prior to this day, I had really been pressing into the Lord about my purpose and what He had called me to do. I knew He called me to do *something*, I just didn't know what it was. I had no idea that in

9

that moment, **He was about to blow my mind with the plans that He had for my life.**

After turning off the TV, He told me to grab my bible and journal—I grabbed both and said, "Well Lord, speak to me. What do you want me to know?"

"*My daughter, I love you so much. My love for you is great.* (I love that whenever God speaks to me, He usually starts off saying that. How reassuring!) *I have called you to preach the gospel of Jesus Christ. You and your husband will travel this world and preach, and millions of people will come into the knowledge of me through the ministry I will give you. Don't be afraid to travel internationally or get on airplanes. I will protect you and I will be with you.*"

Wait, what Lord? Me?! I am at an internship to become a TV producer! Well, I jumped up and ran to tell my roommate (who wasn't saved at the time) what the Lord called me to do! I was so excited. In that moment, she gave me this weird look, "Preacher? We are here to be producers!" It was in that moment, walking back to my room with my head down, the Lord said to me, "*Heather, everybody isn't going to understand what I have called you to do. That is why I told you, and not them.*" I quickly learned that I cannot let people ruffle my feathers, especially when I know that I am being obedient to the Lord. What a test of people bondage!

It was on that day, in the Fall of 2003, where I truly started this beautiful journey of faith. The Lord continued to show me that I would not see the fruit of what He called me to do for some time. Crazy, right? I didn't see an actual stage for nine years after that moment in my apartment. **Many times we can know what God called us to do, we just don't have the character to sustain us in our purpose**. Plainly put, *I wasn't ready*. It's not even that I wanted a stage, because my heart was simply to serve the Lord; it was that God still needed to develop me because I just wasn't ready.

If I had my current portion ten years ago, it would have crushed me. I was still in people bondage, and I cared what people thought of me in an unhealthy way. I was still very insecure and confused about life, still kept a boyfriend that I wasn't supposed to be with, argued with God pretty often, and I just didn't always make good decisions. I truly in my heart didn't walk by faith and trust God. I sang the songs, I went to the bible studies, but my heart was still led by the flesh, and not His spirit. Many of us are making these same mistakes; **trying to birth children in the first trimester of our pregnancy**. Yes, you've just become pregnant with that purpose, but it's not the time or the season to see those things come to pass. Then, out of fear, we begin to compare our pregnancy to someone who just gave birth to their child.

I heard a story once about a dog and an elephant that became pregnant at the same time. Three months down the line, the dog gave birth to six puppies. Six months later, the dog was pregnant again, but this time, gave birth to a dozen puppies, and the pattern continued. Upon the eighteenth month, the dog approached the elephant questioning, "Are you sure that you are pregnant? We became pregnant at the same time; yet, I have given birth three times to more than a dozen puppies and they have grown to become big dogs, but you are still pregnant. What's going on?" The elephant replied, "What I am carrying is not a puppy, but an elephant. It takes two years to develop him to term. When my baby hits the ground, the earth feels it. When my baby crosses the road, human beings stop and watch in admiration. What I'm carrying is mighty and great."

It's not that the elephant was better than the puppies, they just served a different purpose. Just because someone else walks into their purpose before you, doesn't mean that we should get envious or jealous of them. Your time will come, but complaining and coveting their life, purpose, and puppies, surely won't make your purpose come any faster.

Let's bring this a little closer to home, "Oh Lord, how is it that so and so just started her ministry, and it seems like it's growing faster than mine? Why Lord!?" "Why is it that my coworker received the promotion and I work harder than she does?" "Why this, why that Lord?" What a waste of time! This is why the Lord assures us in Ecclesiastes 3:1, "For everything there is a season, a time for every activity under heaven." He says this because we question the **"for everything."** "What about my job? What about my man? When am I going to have those kids I keep seeing in my dreams? When is this gonna happen? Lord, when is that?" We run to prophet-lyers, psychics, online dating websites, and everything else under the sun to find our "for everything," and all the while, the Lord is saying, *"Trust Me. Trust Me. Trust Me."*

Don't trust your degree because if you haven't noticed, this world trusts their degrees and unemployment is at an all time high. Don't even trust in your job, because what happens when there are layoffs next week, or you lose that promotion you just prayed for? Some of you think that when you lose a job, a person, or are struggling with college, that you're on the wrong path. No! When you're living for the Lord, it simply means that He is directing your path. Why would a great Father allow you to go through a door that you are not supposed to enter? As a mother of two children, I am constantly seeking their best interest. I am constantly watching over them. As earthly as I am, it makes me consider the Lord; He knows the hearts of all people and the "opportunities" that we should not consider because He knows what is on the other side of it all.

Some of you may have been pregnant with things that were artificial, or trying to force his will by attempting to give birth to gifts and talents he never approved of. Then, you get upset and mad at God because you don't feel fulfilled as a Doctor, or because you just got laid off from your job. All the while, the Lord is saying, *"I didn't tell you to pursue those things."* For years, your ladder has been leaning up against the wrong building while God is saying, "Yes, I know that you thought you were going to make all of this money at that job, but I am trying to teach you to trust in Me, and not money."

This journey of faith calls for us to simply put one

foot in front of the other, and I hope the personal stories I share about how God developed my purpose, will encourage you to boldly step into what God has for you too.

Chapter 2:

What are you

afraid of?

Ask yourself these two questions: What do you believe God has called you to do? And, what is keeping you from doing that very thing?

After asking these questions to hundreds of women over the years, the main answer I get is fear—the fear of failing, fear of taking the first step, and the fear of money.

WHAT IS FEAR?

The Bible mentions two different types of fear. The first type is beneficial and is to be encouraged, which is the fear of the Lord. The second type is of this world, and it is to be avoided. Fear of the Lord is a reverential awe of God; a reverence for His power and glory. However, it is also a respect for His wrath and anger. In other words, the fear of the Lord is a total acknowledgement of all that God is, which comes through knowing Him and His attributes. It's a respect that says, "Lord, I love, fear and reverence you so much that I will no longer pursue sin, or chase after what this world offers me." Thus, one can see why fearing God should be encouraged.

The second type of fear mentioned in the Bible is not beneficial. This is the "spirit of fear" mentioned in

2 Timothy 1:7, which says, "For God has not given us a spirit of fear and timidity, but of power, love, and self-discipline." A spirit of fearfulness and timidity does not come from God. For example, in Isaiah 41:10 the Word says, *"Do not fear, for I am with you; Do not anxiously look about you, for I am your God I will strengthen you, surely I will help you, Surely I will uphold you with My righteous right hand."*

Most times, we fear the future and what will become of us. We wonder if we step out on faith, whether God is going to provide and take care of us. But Jesus reminds us that God cares for the birds of the air, so how much more will He provide for His children? *"So don't be afraid; you are worth more than many sparrows (Matthew 10:31)."*

God tells us not to be afraid of being alone, of being too weak, of not being heard, of lacking physical necessities, and so much more. There is an answer in the word of God that contradicts every fear that is stirring in your heart! As I mentioned earlier, that fear didn't come from the Lord, and because it didn't, that means it came from the enemy, Satan. He is roaring around like a lion, looking for those he can destroy (1 Peter 5:8). If he can keep you *afraid* of doing what God called you to do, you will never be in alignment with God's purpose for your life. Instead, you will hide under your gifts and talents your entire life, wondering what "could have, should have, or would have happened," if you were obedient to the Lord.

Whenever I become afraid of something, I am directly telling God that *I do not trust Him*. There's no way that full trust and fear can live in the same home. One of them will always trump the other depending on your mindset. In Psalm 56:11 it says, "*In God I trust; I will not be afraid. What can man do to me?*" This is an awesome testimony to the power of trusting in God. Regardless of what happens, David says that He will trust in God because he knows, and understands the power of the Lord. The key, then, to overcoming fear, **is total and complete trust in God.** Trusting God is a refusal to give in to fear. It's a refusal to place your trust in this world. It's a refusal to just do something to do it, because you don't trust that God will take care of you. It is turning to God even in the darkest times and trusting Him to make things right.

This trust comes from knowing God and knowing that He is good. How do we really learn to trust God? By spending time with Him consistently and stepping out on faith. You don't trust someone that you don't know, but after becoming comfortable in who He is and as you continue to step out on faith, you are going to find that He will absolutely blow your mind as you let Him lead you! When you don't spend quality time sitting at His feet, reading your bible, or being intentional about applying what you've learned, distrust of God will develop in your heart—causing your heart to be hardened against Him.

Spending time with the Lord will give you perspective! It will keep you close to the Lord so when fear attacks you, you can remind Satan and all of his little demons that you are not led by a spirit of fear, but you are led by the Lord who gives you a boldness and a faith to do what you have been called to do. Once we honestly put our trust in the Lord, we will no longer be afraid of the attacks that come our way.

Let's look at some of Satan's common attacks on keeping us from living in our purpose:

THE FEAR OF FAILING

Sister, let's sit down for this one. I'm going to look you in the face and tell you the truth. The truth is that you are either going to fear failing, or you are going to fear God.

"But Heather, I fear both."

Sis, one day you will stand before Jesus Christ and you will have to give an account for what you were supposed to do on this earth. What will you say to Jesus when you meet Him face to face? You are only a heartbeat away from meeting Him. Jesus took care of the fear of failure because accomplishing our purpose is through Him and not through you. If you fear failing, then you are proving that you trust in yourself more than you do God's ability. We have to get our eyes off of our ability, our ways, our past, and anything else holding us back. We cannot hold on to the excuses that we are not "whatever enough" because God is saying that through me you can do all things. "Why do we have so little faith (Matthew 8:26)?"

Honestly, I have been there. Even in ministry now, I get attacked with thoughts of inferiority, and negativity like, "Nobody wants to read your books Heather, nobody will attend your conferences. Why don't you just quit all together and stop speaking?"

You know what I tell those thoughts from Satan? I tell him that I didn't ask him what he thought about my purpose. I didn't ask him what he thought of my sermon. I didn't ask him to come to my conferences, so why are you speaking to me? You do not have permission. I have the mind of Christ (1 Corinthians 2:16)! I belong to Jesus! I won't entertain your lies, your thoughts, your suggestions and your opinion. If you meet someone that constantly lies to you, and they have never told you the truth, at some point you become wise enough to not go back down that road. That person has proved to be untrustworthy. Same goes for Satan. He has proven to be a liar and we should not entertain him.

FEAR OF TAKING THE FIRST STEP

Gosh, I can totally relate. I felt the same exact way. I knew that I liked helping women, accessories, and I loved gathering people together to share Jesus—I wanted to incorporate all three, but I didn't know how to do it. Guess what? You won't either.

We won't know until God shows us. Isn't that amazing? God says to you, "I started this work in you and I will complete it (Philippians 1:6)." If God hasn't made things clear to you or you don't know all the answers, don't get uptight about it, because He will complete what He has started! He will show you at the appointed time. Now, if you aren't pursuing Him, He's not going to just open doors and give you your heart's desire because you will ruin your witness, and if you ignore God, you aren't ready for a huge calling anyway. You can't desire your purpose and continually live in your sin. You aren't serving Jesus, but yourself and your father, the devil (1 John). If you are seriously pursuing Christ and no longer pursuing sin, I can assure you that God will show you what He wants you to do.

He told me step one, to start writing "notes" on social media platforms. Then, He told me to blog at a time where people weren't really blogging about Christianity. A year later, He instructed me to make a bracelet. To others, that may not make sense but I didn't get the next step to start an organization until I was obedient with the first steps that He told me to take. So, I ask you, are you being faithful with the first thing the Lord told you to do? Were you obedient when He told you to cut that person off, to leave that job, to move to another state, to spend time with Him daily, to stop overspending, or whatever else? There are levels to our relationship with Jesus. Many times we want the full manifestation of what God has called us to do without sacrificing anything. We want what we want. Let's instead want what He wants for our lives, even if that means we have to do it without our "feel good emotions" catching up.

FEAR OF FINANCIAL INSTABILITY

"Heather, how am I going to eat?"

"How am I going to do what God called me to do, and step out on faith with limited money?"

You may be the sole income in your home, a stay at home mama, helping to support your household, or you could be a single person that is trying to figure out how to pay your cell phone bill every month. Regardless of where God has placed you in your current season, why is money stopping you from doing what God has called you to do?

The amazing thing about God is that He chooses us for a purpose, and He takes care of us. About a month ago, the Lord told me to plant a garden. I did what I was told, and went all out with it. I found a garden box from a specialty store and I built it outside in our backyard. I added dirt, worms, and seeds, and I constantly kept an eye on it. The Lord then told me to walk around the corner to a shaded part of my yard, and plant cucumbers in the corner in a clay-dirt foundation. The Lord told me to plant this way to gain understanding for this book, so I planted away without having all the answers. In one area, the garden pod has the perfect soil, great sunlight, perfect fertilizer, worms, gets watered daily and I'm constantly watching over it; where as, the cucumber plant was planted in clay-dirt and has not been touched since the day it was planted.

What's my point?

The garden pod represents the person that seems to have life handed to them—a great family, didn't want for anything, flourished because their family knew to teach them about Christ, protected them, connected them, and took care of them. Nothing wrong with this person as I'm sure they had to deal with some of their own weeds. The lone plant represents the person who has struggled greatly, didn't have the best foundation growing up, a broken family, saw a lot of dysfunction, was never taken care of, and most times forgotten and overlooked. Both people matter, and both people are important, but do you know that lone plant is flourishing just as well as the other plants? The cucumber plant was created with the purpose of thriving with little assistance. The same applies to God's children—when God starts a work in *you*, He will complete it, so stop comparing your cucumber plant to the garden pod!

When God formed you in your mother's womb, He didn't ask you how much money you would make when you became a certain age. He doesn't ask about your potential education, or what your parents do for a living, instead He plants purpose in your heart. That lone plant is going to grow as long as it's connected to the vine, Jesus Christ. That's the beautiful thing about living for Jesus! He anoints and chooses whoever He wishes and it has nothing to do with what this world thinks of you.

Any gardener would plant the vegetables and fruits in a garden box, not in a clay-dirt foundation. Some of you have been written off by a gardener. You've been written off by a teacher. A parent. A friend. An ex boyfriend. A mentor. You have been thrown to the side of the yard, and you may feel like you have to go into survivor mode. I know your foundation is a little tougher, but God is right there with you, and harvest season is coming if you just hold tight to His word.

I was definitely the lone plant. My family is *more* than supportive, encouraging and loving, but my husband and I are first generation preachers with no official training. We literally have bloomed around the corner, privately, when no one was paying attention. Then, God shined His light on us. I don't know why God has chosen us for this generation, but I am just thankful that He has Included me in His plans. And guess what? Regardless of which plant you are, God has His hands on you as you live for Him.

It doesn't matter if you don't have the right connections, education, money, or whatever else! It doesn't matter if your past was jacked up and you had a bad reputation! When God has His hands on you, you will grow in the midst of your situation, even if you feel forgotten. Hang in there and keep trusting Him regardless of your portion. You have purpose, even if it doesn't feel like it.

When I started Pinky Promise in January of 2012, I was still working from home with a corporate job. I worked in Human Resources, and at night I would preach and make bracelets. At the time, my husband wasn't working because the Lord told him not to—I know, we sound crazy— as the Lord was preparing him for our church, The Gathering Oasis, and ministry in general. I would literally watch him study and pray 8-10 hours a day. Eventually, we both started to get invitations to speaking engagements where we would fly to our destination early in the morning, I would work in the hotel all day, and I would preach at night sessions. Things were getting pretty hectic.

That January, I told my husband that I really wanted to leave my job and that I was tired of doing both. We prayed about it, and had peace about me staying for six more months. I didn't just quit. I just worked on our ministry in my off time. Then, five months later, my boss got fired, and my new supervisor expressed that he wanted me to move back to New York to work out of their offices. Absolutely not. We knew that we were not supposed to move to New York. I told them that I would leave in one month, which was exactly six months after I mentioned to my husband that I felt like my season was coming to an end.

As if that was not enough confirmation, the day my boss told me that I would need to move, the Lord also told us to move back to Atlanta from being in Mississippi for one year. Then, guess what happened the next day? We found out that we were pregnant with Logan! What a test of our faith! Part of me wanted the stability of insurance, a constant paycheck, and whatever else I thought I needed to be satisfied, but God had a different plan for us. We pressed forward through those tests, and soon, the month had come and gone and it was my last day of work! We had been saving a lot, as we only had one income. We thought we were set for a little bit, until the transmission in my truck gave out, and the key for the ignition stopped working. The total for repairs ended up wiping out our savings.

"LORD! What is going on? We are being faithful to you! We are doing what we know to do! We are pregnant and we are trying to save for our children! You have got to help us!" The Lord's response:

"Heather, you had more hope in your savings than you did in Me."

Welp. I mean, you couldn't have just told me that without the transmission going out in the car?

Matthew 6:24 says, "No one can serve two masters. For you will hate one and love the other; you will be devoted to one and despise the other. You cannot serve both God and money."

Sometimes, we need to go through tests to prove our hearts. When the transmission went out, I began to question my purpose. "Maybe, I should have kept the job? Maybe, I should have saved more, maybe this, maybe that." Then, thoughts began to run through my head, "Lord, did I miss you?"

I had to literally *fight back* those thoughts and stand firm in knowing that I was in the will of God for my life. Now, years later, I can boldly stand and confirm that God is truly a great Provider. He has taken care of our family, and we have lacked for nothing. He has been so good to us! This does not mean that we don't get tested, it just means that we've passed the test of putting our trust in our finances. We walk by faith and do whatever God tells us to do because God provides for his children. Period.

Months after stepping out in faith, I learned that the business I worked for had massive layoffs where most of the company was let go—including most of my department and my old position. If we would have packed up and moved to New York City for my job, or money, then we would have been stuck a month later. I was pregnant so it would have been difficult to get another job, and we would have literally had to start all over. I am so glad that we trusted in the Lord to take care of us, and left when He told us to.

I have learned that as we build ourselves up in faith, we get challenged with even bigger financial tests, but now, we are so used to passing them, that we don't even think about it. We look at the amount that is due and laugh as we tell the Lord that we trust Him—and, every single time He has provided for us. We *needed* those small tests to learn to trust God in the area of being our Provider.

Sis, you have to start somewhere. You are not all of a sudden going to have the faith to step out and leave what is comfortable to you. **God develops us in seasons**! He may tell you to give someone $10 on the street and tell them that God loves them. He may tell you to buy groceries for a single mother. He may tell you to walk up to someone and tell them that God has not forgotten about them. Just obey Him in small things, and your faith will grow! You literally have to practice hearing the voice of the Lord. We go from faith to faith. Glory to glory! Don't let a piece of paper (money) be the reason that you do not obey the Lord! He is so much greater than money!

Making the decision to step out on faith into the unknown, even without knowing where the money will come from, is what the Lord requires of us—that's the beautiful thing about God. He gives us step one, then, after taking that first leap of faith, He gives further instructions. We just have to trust him completely, even if he doesn't deliver until the "last hour." In the midst of seeking out your own purpose, it's important that you don't compare your faith walk to other people's story because there is no formula to accomplishing the will of God for your life. It's simply you putting one foot in front of the other and deciding to trust Him by faith.

Chapter 3:
Crying over
spilled milk

One day, in my prayer room, I heard this crashing sound from the kitchen. I go downstairs and see my freshly pumped, seven-ounce bottle of breast milk spilled all over the floor. My liquid gold is everywhere. Two days earlier, the exact same thing happened; I literally wanted to scream. I was preparing to travel out of town, and was trying to store up milk for the trip. I looked at the beautiful wasted milk, and literally felt every emotion. If you are a breastfeeding mama, you know that you have to work hard for those ounces. I wanted to scream, to yell, to ask why, how, when, and a million other questions. Instead, I turned around and walked right back upstairs. What would yelling and screaming over spilled milk do?

Has something happened in your life and it's already done? I mean, the milk is on the ground, the situation has passed, the relationship has ended, the abortion is done, the job has come and gone, the past is there, but what are you going to do with it? **Are you going to sit and stress out about spilled milk, or are you going to get up and do what Jesus is calling you to do?** You cannot let the past, even if it happened a few moments ago, control you. What is done, is done, and what happened, happened, and now it's time to move forward. I was going to sit there and let the spilled milk ruin my day, which may sound silly, but some of us let our past and situations ruin our entire lives.

We allow ourselves to be paralyzed in fear, which keeps us from stepping out on faith. We don't pursue Jesus with our whole heart, we don't rest in the Lord, and we don't fully trust Him, or what He has called us to do. When He sends a Godly man, we run him off because of our past hurt, and we charge him for what people did in the past. Or, maybe you're married and you allow all of your hurts from family or whatever you've seen in the past, frame your thinking. Now we figure, since so and so got divorced and couldn't make it, maybe we won't make it either. When Jesus sends Godly friends, we think they are out to get us, and we push them away. When Jesus sends us a job, we become inferior and insecure because of the way we see ourselves.

If you see yourself in this at all, I want to remind you of Philippians 3:13:

"No, dear brothers and sisters, I have not achieved it, but I focus on this one thing: Forgetting the past and looking forward to what lies ahead, I press on to

reach the end of the race and receive the heavenly prize for which God, through Christ Jesus, is calling us."

What is your focus? Is it what happened in the past, or is it looking forward to what lies ahead? God is saying, "Yes, these things happened to you. Yes, they were hard. Yes, you made some not so great decisions, but you have to stop holding onto those things as a crutch!"

"So now there is no condemnation for those who belong to Christ Jesus. And because you belong to him, the power of the life-giving Spirit has freed you from the power of sin that leads to death."
- Romans 8:1-2

Repent of your past decisions. Stop rolling over in your mind what could have happened, should have happened, or whatever else. Many times, we go back over in our heads and wonder whether things would have worked out if we did something different. Who knows? What we do know is that you made that decision, and now it's time to press forward to what Jesus has called you to do. Let go of the spilled milk. Clean it up off the floor, throw the towel in the garbage, and pray that God restores your milk supply.

Ask the Holy Spirit to cleanse your heart and repent of your past ways. Stop going back and forth with yourself. Do you know that these things are a direct attack on your future and what God has called you to do? If Satan can get you to not feel good about yourself, it will wreck your confidence and keep you from trusting in the Lord. You will begin to doubt Him and question whether God loves you, or if He really has a plan for you. It's *all* an attack against doing what God has called you to do! If you feel like crap, you are going to continue in what is comfortable. I will just work this same job for 35 years until I retire, but deep down, you know God has called you to something else. We have to stop crying over spilled milk! We have to stop allowing our past to keep us from where God is taking us! We have to let it go!

If this is you, I encourage you to put this book down and go pray. Go to the Lord and give Him your spilled milk. Go home, leave your phone outside of the room, turn on some worship music, and just vent out to the Lord. Cry out to Him. Tell Him that your past has been holding you back from what He has called you to do! Tell Him that you are crippled spiritually. Tell Him that you desperately need direction, help, peace, and joy. Tell Him that you will walk by faith, and not by sight! Tell Him that you are afraid to totally trust Him! The beautiful thing about all of this is that He already knows these things. He just wants you to *"Cast your care upon Him because He cares for you (1 Peter 5:7)."* He is supposed to take on your care!

You know what amazes me about Jesus? He uses unschooled, ordinary people like me and you! I've shared my story many times, but I definitely shouldn't be here—I was supposed to be aborted. Instead, I was adopted into a really amazing family at five months, went on to develop normally, and eventually to graduate from Michigan State University. I had no clue what I was doing, or where God was taking me. I never had a background in theology, but I also learned that I didn't need one, because I knew Him personally.

"The members of the council were amazed when they saw the boldness of Peter and John, for they could see that they were ordinary men with no special training in the Scriptures. They also recognized them as men who had been with Jesus."- Acts 4:13

How cool is this? These disciples were close with Jesus and they spent a lot of time with Him. They were bold for the Lord because they *knew* Him. Guess what? You can be BOLD for the Lord and knowledgeable about scriptures because you spend time with the Author of the Bible. Isn't it amazing that you don't have to be this special type of person to be used by God? You just have to be willing. You just have to be surrendered to Him and flexible. Flexible meaning, "God, whatever thy will is – may it be done according to your Word."

You no longer chase after cars, big houses, ungodly relationships, or past hurts. Instead, ask God to take your spilled milk. Take your life. Take your hurts, your pains, your worry, and your fear. Confess that you will no longer cry over your past. Sis, at some point, you have to leave it there and press forward to what God has called you to do! Do you know if I cried over spilled milk, I would not be writing this book! I would not be preaching to women! I would not have Pinky Promise! I would not accomplish anything! I would literally hide myself, and do nothing out of embarrassment of what people thought of me.

I am quite confident that people from my past are looking at my life now in complete shock. I used to dent up my ex boyfriend's car with my heels because he was cheating on me. I was a certified crazy-stalker girlfriend. I used to cuss out girls that were talking to him. I used to make up curse words, and talk crazy to people. I was such a broken soul. **But, the Lord changed me**. He put a new song in my mouth. He restored me. He changed my spirit. He gave me compassion, strength, and love. He developed me. He did this beautiful work in me.

"..But Heather, the past still hurts."

Well, as I write this, I am still thinking about those seven ounces that were on my kitchen floor, but you know what I have to do? I must press past my feelings:

1. I tell my emotions to get it together. Just because you feel that way, doesn't mean that you have to act out on it. My prayer? Lord, arrest my emotions and make them captive to You (2 Corinthians 10:5).

2. Don't entertain the enemy's thoughts of negativity. We have to remember that this fight is *spiritual*, not physical.

3. After you've vented to the Lord and made your peace, stop replaying what happened over and over again. It's only going to make you even more upset, and you will waste even more days worrying about something that is temporary.

4. Joshua 1:8 tells us to "Study this Book of Instruction continually. Meditate on it day and night so you will be sure to obey everything written in it. Only then will you prosper and succeed in all you do." You can either meditate on the spilled milk, or the frustration, or you can press into Christ.

5. Submit your feelings to the Lord daily by stirring yourself up in the Word. I'm encouraged by David who found joy in the Lord when he was down (Psalm 35:20). I also like to speak these things unto myself: "Heather, you are more than a conqueror through Christ Jesus! You are not some little wimpy girl! God has a plan for you, and this test is maturing and developing you from the milk of the Word to the meat of the Word! Don't you dare stop holding onto

the Lord! Don't you dare give up! Don't you dare quit! You are not going around this mountain anymore! It stops today!!"

I have learned that it's not that the feelings and tests go away, it's just that I've learned to develop past their ability to hurt me. I'm no longer the wimpy little girl I once was. The Lord has strengthened me. **The tests and the spilled milk have made me better.** My past has made me better. It's made me rely on the Lord for every single part of my life. It's made me a barefooted priest. It's made me free from the opinions of people so I can pursue Christ wholeheartedly, despite how uncomfortable it may feel at times.

Not long after my milk was spilled on the floor, I went on to pump 10 ounces in 15 minutes! I wonder how many times God plans on giving us more for what we think we lost, but we are too afraid to let go? The milk was used as a lesson to show me I cannot control everything that happens, but I can control my response. I can choose to wake up everyday and live for Jesus. I can choose to trust Him. I can choose to not quit. Rest my love, God takes care of all of the other stuff. There's something on the other side of the spilled milk.

So, where has God placed you right now? Are you in a state of endurance, where you must look to the Father, and not at the milk that has spilled all over your floor? There's a reason for it.

Chapter 4:

Where has God

placed you now?

I sense in my spirit that some of you are at jobs that you absolutely hate, and you're ready to leave them to run and do something else. I want you to know that running from job to job, school to school, or the next, is not going to bring you closer to what God called you to do. Instead, that **same challenging personality or test is going to meet you at your next location.** I can recall experiencing extremely difficult personalities everywhere I worked while in New York City. Every boss I worked for had intense, Type-A personalities, that called for my work to be very detailed oriented. They gave me no grace, and they were very hard on me. Not only did I work with difficult bosses, but I barely got paid while doing it.

I was so jealous of my co-workers who seemed to get along perfectly with their bosses, and here I am just trying to survive. In retrospect, I am thankful that my bosses were hard on me. Why? I needed those tough situations because I was an emotional wimpy train wreck. How can I have this worldwide ministry one day if I cannot overcome working with a difficult employer? Working for these kinds of bosses strengthened me and developed me. Did I cry? Um... Yes! Did I ask God to quit everyday? You bet I did. Did I have rough moments? Of course! There were times where I had to go to the bathroom and cry my eyes out because I was so frustrated with my job. I was being treated harshly *and* I was about to get evicted—talk about stressful!

I was drained emotionally and physically throughout this hectic time, but I always made sure to spend time with the Lord every morning and night. I wanted to make sure that I was so in tune to His voice, that I could leave the second that He gave me permission to. I didn't want to be cluttered in my spirit even in the midst of my frustration.

So, where has God placed you right now? Are you frustrated to the point where you want to quit? Do you see yourself as frustrated like I was with my old position? Do you feel like you have no purpose at your job or that you're not "moving up" in the company? Remember, as we live for Jesus, it's Him alone that opens and closes our doors. If you're not getting the recognition you think you deserve, it's not time to jump ship. It's not time to leave. It's not time to search for another job. It's time for you to go and sit before the Lord, and leave when He tells you to leave.

When trusting in the Lord, much faith is required and it sometimes means that we stay in uncomfortable places until the Lord tells us to move.

The Lord told me to leave at a certain time, because that was when it was time to go. I put in my two-weeks notice, but my boss suggested I stay and just work with another supervisor; someone who would be less demanding. So, I stayed for three more months than I believed I was supposed to be there, even though I knew my time was up. Out of nowhere, my new bosses said that they were doing layoffs and I was included. Was I supposed to be included? No, I wasn't even supposed to be there. Eventually, my temp company assigned me to another short term position, and I took the job until I could figure out what was next.

I can recall sitting at a computer screen, dressed professionally, in a super tiny cubicle that faced the wall. I said, "Lord, you've called me for something so much greater. I feel like I went from working a crazy busy job, to staring at a computer screen, and doing data entry work. I know that you have called me to this world-wide ministry, I just don't know how I am going to get there at this dead end job, doing data entry work, in business casual attire." As I vented my frustrations to the Lord, I realized that I had placed my worth in this world. Even though I stepped out on faith with my old job, and put the bug in their ear that I didn't want to be there without anything lined up, **I still felt purposeless**.

Later, the Lord revealed to me that I needed to know that my worth came from Him alone, and not a job, a person, a degree or anything else. Even though I was sitting at a computer screen in that small cubicle, God birthed such a huge *purpose* in me. It was the first trimester in my "purpose pregnancy." You couldn't see any proof that I had purpose, but it was simply a matter of time before God opened that door.

You may not be where you want to be in your life—you may hate your job, you may feel purposeless, but I want you to know that it is not by chance that you stumbled across this book. The Lord has sent me here to remind you that *you* have a purpose. *You* have a plan. I don't care if your parents said that you were a mistake, or if everyone else has written you off. I don't care if you don't feel pretty based on the world's standards. I don't care if you don't see it; none of these things matter. The only thing that matters is while you were in your mother's womb, God gave you purpose. He had you in mind when He created the heavens and the earth. There's a reason that you were born at the time in which you were. The Lord sent you here to this earth to solve a specific purpose. You are no accident and God desires to use you today—right in your cubicle, or as you change those diapers, or on your commute to work. He wants every single moment. Do you give your moments to Him, or are you too distracted and too busy with your life that you don't have time to sit before the Father and let Him instruct you?

No wonder why you hate your job so much! No wonder you don't feel good about yourself! The foundation to these things is contentment in Jesus Christ. It's placing your hope and trust in Him, and Him alone—not this crazy world.

This world will have you so confused chasing after it's approval. The story of Joseph is a perfect example of this:

"When Joseph was seventeen years old, he often tended his father's flocks. He worked for his half brothers, the sons of his father's wives Bilhah and Zilpah. But Joseph reported to his father some of the bad things his brothers were doing.Jacob loved Joseph more than any of his other children because Joseph had been born to him in his old age. So one day, Jacob had a special gift made for Joseph—a beautiful

robe. *But his brothers hated Joseph because their father loved him more than the rest of them. They couldn't say a kind word to him.*

One night, Joseph had a dream, and when he told his brothers about it, they hated him more than ever. 'Listen to this dream,' he said. 'We were out in the field, tying up bundles of grain. Suddenly my bundle stood up, and your bundles all gathered around and bowed low before mine!'

His brothers responded, 'So you think you will be our king, do you? Do you actually think you will reign over us?' And they hated him all the more because of his dreams and the way he talked about them." -Genesis 37: 2-8

Do you have any "brothers," or people talking about you, or doubting the vision God has given you? Maybe you are sharing what God has called you to do with others, and they don't believe in it. Maybe they are in a position of authority, and look down on you. These people don't like your confidence, your boldness, your love for Jesus, and your trust in Him. Your trust in Jesus actually intimidates them, and challenges them at the same time. It challenges them because they don't have your faith, and it makes them feel inferior. Is it your fault? Of course not! It's up to them to develop a relationship with Jesus for themselves, and prayerfully by watching your example, they will do so. Let's keep reading.

"Soon Joseph had another dream, and again he told his brothers about it. 'Listen, I have had another dream,' he said. 'The sun, moon, and eleven stars bowed low before me!' This time he told the dream to his father as well as to his brothers, but his father scolded him. 'What kind of dream is that?' he asked. 'Will your mother and I and your brothers actually come and bow to the ground before you?' But while his brothers were jealous of Joseph, his father wondered what the dreams meant. Soon after this, Joseph's brothers went to pasture their father's flocks at Shechem. When they had been gone for some time, Jacob said to Joseph, 'Your brothers are pasturing the sheep at Shechem. Get ready, and I will send you to them.' 'I'm ready to go,' Joseph replied.

'Go and see how your brothers and the flocks are getting along,' Jacob said. 'Then come back and bring me a report.' So Jacob sent him on his way, and Joseph traveled to Shechem from their

home in the valley of Hebron. When he arrived there, a man from the area noticed him wandering around the countryside. 'What are you looking for?' he asked.

'I'm looking for my brothers,' Joseph replied. 'Do you know where they are pasturing their sheep?' 'Yes,' the man told him. 'They have moved on from here, but I heard them say, 'Let's go on to Dothan.'' So Joseph followed his brothers to Dothan and found them there.

When Joseph's brothers saw him coming, they recognized him in the distance. As he approached, they made plans to kill him."
- Genesis 37: 9-18

Joseph's brothers were so jealous of him, that they wanted to kill him! Maybe you have people around you that want you out of the way. It could be a family member, or a co-worker; maybe it's someone who is always talking down to you, or someone who is constantly "throwing you under the bus." No matter who tries to get you fired or out of proper position, when God has His hand on you, His plan is all that matters.

"'Here comes the dreamer!' they said. 'Come on, let's kill him and throw him into one of these cisterns. We can tell our father, 'A wild animal has eaten him.' Then we'll see what becomes of his dreams!'"

"But when Reuben heard of their scheme, he came to Joseph's rescue. 'Let's not kill him," he said. "Why should we shed any blood? Let's just throw him into this empty cistern here in the wilderness. Then he'll die without our laying a hand on him.' Reuben was secretly planning to rescue Joseph and return him to his father. So when Joseph arrived, his brothers ripped off the beautiful robe he was wearing. Then they grabbed him and threw him into the cistern. Now the cistern was empty, there was no water in it. Then, just as they were sitting down to eat, they looked up and saw a caravan of camels in the distance coming toward them. It was a group of Ishmaelite traders taking a load of gum, balm, and aromatic resin from Gilead down to Egypt.

Judah said to his brothers, "What will we gain by killing our brother? We'd have to cover up the crime. Instead of hurting him, let's sell him to those Ishmaelite traders. After all, he is our brother—our own flesh and blood!" And his *brothers agreed. So when the Ishmaelites, who were Midianite traders, came by, Joseph's brothers pulled him out of the cistern and sold him to them for twenty pieces of silver. And the traders took him to Egypt." - Genesis 37: 19-27*

If you're feeling like Joseph in his younger days when he was getting attacked left and right, I want to say, "Welcome to the club!" Joseph had to learn a lesson in contentment. He had to learn that no matter what he was experiencing externally, He must trust God. God's very purpose for Joseph was to be set apart and to be made king. I am confident that Joseph felt like the Lord may have forgotten about him, and I am sure he doubted God here and there.

You may assume that just because I have a ministry, and I write books, that I don't get attacked with thoughts of insufficiency; that I don't wonder whether God will come through, or feeling like what I do is purposeless, or like I'm not enough while wondering, "God, *why* did you call me?" I get attacked with these feelings and thoughts just like every other believer. I, too, question the very call on my life. But, what do I do? I refuse to sit and entertain those thoughts because I know that they don't come from the *Father*. Those thoughts come from

Satan himself, and I'm not interested in talking to someone that has no authority to talk to me.

Since Satan has no authority over me, I talk *down* to him and say, "Philippians 1:6 tells me that God started this work in me, not you. And because God started this work in me, He will complete it. I said, He will complete it. Since you're a liar Satan, you obviously don't understand that 'complete' means having all necessary parts, not lacking anything, or being limited in any way!"

"God completing this work in me means that my purpose won't lack a single thing. I am not limited in any way. My purpose does not require your demonic opinion, or any of your demons roaming around this work trying to destroy what the Lord has started in me. Try to use Joseph's brothers and whoever else against me— It won't work. Matter of fact, you have to get permission from my God in order to even test me. Which further tells me that you cannot test me outside of the Lord's will (Job 1:12). Because I know this to be true, I recognize this: *'And we know that God causes everything to work together for the good of those who love God and are called according to his purpose for them (Romans 8:28).'"*

So, what happened to Joseph?

He was bought by an Egyptian of high rank, Potiphar, and through his good character, eventually gained a high position in his household. One day, Potiphar's wife tried to seduce Joseph and came on to him very strongly. He resisted her, and ran away. She was embarrassed that Joseph refused her out of loyalty to Potiphar, so she lied to her husband; telling him that it was Joseph who tried to seduce her. Joseph was then thrown in jail.

Can you imagine how he must have been feeling? Have you ever felt like you were doing the right thing and still got persecuted, or that you kept getting the "short end of the stick" in a situation? You may think that Joseph's life was over, but in Genesis 39:2 it says that the Lord was with Joseph and He prospered wherever he went.

While in prison, Joseph met two men who worked in Potiphar's household—the chief butler and baker—of whom, he had successfully interpreted their dreams.

Eventually they leave the jail—the baker to be hanged, the butler to return to work, which was the fulfillment of their dreams—and Joseph is forgotten about. Some time later, Potiphar is plagued by disturbing dreams which he cannot remember upon waking. His wise men cannot help him since they don't know what the dreams are, and eventually the butler remembers Joseph's skill with dreams and recommends him to Potiphar.

Joseph is called from the jail and through prayer is able to tell Potiphar what his dreams were *and* the interpretation. The dreams were a warning of 7 years of bountiful crops, followed by 7 years of famine. Potiphar was pleased that Joseph interpreted the dreams, and put him in charge of storing away crops for the first 7 years so that there will be enough to last Egypt through the 7 years of famine. Joseph becomes very important and is the second most important person after Potiphar.

Second in command! Every rejection, every moment, every tear, every frustration prepared him for this moment where God would use him to be second in command in Egypt. We as believers get tested with small things and we run from them because we are afraid, or we don't understand. What if Joseph just quit after being thrown in jail? What if he doubted God's ability through him to interpret dreams? Then, he wouldn't see what was on the other side of his obedience.

During the 7 years of famine Joseph's brothers came to Egypt to purchase grain for their family.

Joseph recognizes them, but doesn't reveal his identity—this of course is the fulfillment of Joseph's dreams years ago, where he dreamed that his brothers would bow to him. He invites them to dine with him while they're there, and secretly has something valuable stowed away in the bags of grain they bought.

As they leave, he has guards chase after them and accuse them of stealing. When their bags of grain are searched, the stolen object is found. Joseph accuses them of being spies, not innocent brothers coming for grain. They protest and Joseph says he'll believe them if they return home and bring their youngest brother Benjamin, who was only a baby when Joseph last saw him, as proof that they are his brothers. He keeps one of his brothers hostage until the others return with Benjamin. They do, and he repeats the same scheme, hiding stolen goods in their bags; this time he demands to keep Benjamin as a slave as payment.

Judah, the oldest brother, intercedes and offers his own life as a slave instead of Benjamin. Joseph sees the love his brothers have for Benjamin and for their father, who loves Benjamin dearly, and he confesses to them who he is. They ask forgiveness for what they did to Joseph so long ago, and he tells them it's okay because God has worked it all out for good. The brothers return home and then bring their families and their father back to Egypt.

God can use horrible circumstances for good. Because Joseph was obedient and remained in the place God wanted him, despite it being uncomfortable, he was able to use his skills to protect a whole nation, and his brothers, from a terrible famine. He was even able to reconcile with his family after so many years. **This shows us that we don't need to know the result of our obedience to remain in the particular space God has called us.**

Despite your co-workers, God can use you. Despite your upbringing, God can use you. Despite what others think of you, God can use you. Despite what it looks like, God can use you! Even if you went to jail, even if you were accused wrongfully, even if you don't feel like you can make it. For years, I had to stir myself up in the Lord, and say these things out loud to myself. I would stare in the mirror during my quiet time and tell myself that I had worth and value because of Jesus. I have purpose because I choose Jesus. I am not my past sins or mistakes! I have been redeemed by the precious blood of Jesus! Sis, don't entertain Satan's lies! Joseph used every setback by remaining consistent and close to the Lord! It prepared him for his calling! God is preparing you for your calling but you have to guard your heart.

You must talk back to the enemy who is trying to ruin your mindset! Say this with me, "I have the mind of Christ!" Stir yourself up in the Lord!

"Heather, really? How can my bad situations be good based on what you just said?" Love, it doesn't mean that all that happens to us is good. Evil is prevalent in this fallen world, but God is able to turn every circumstance around for our good in the long run! We must learn to be comfortable with not knowing the answer. Comfortable with our quiet season. Comfortable in knowing that God is not working to make us happy, but to fulfill His purpose.

Chapter 5:

What is your

Purpose?

While sitting in a tea shop in Atlanta, I was watching people walk by, and couldn't help but wonder if they **felt trapped in their uniform.** Whether it's their work uniform, dress suit and heels, or school backpack, I couldn't help but wonder if they were truly in position of where God called them to be. I also wondered what this world would be like if every person on this earth was either in the process of getting to where God called them to be, working as unto the Lord, or actually walking in their purpose.

You could be in two places in your life right now: simply developing where the Lord has planted you, or you could be somewhere that you are not supposed to be. I've been in both. I recall taking an executive assistant job that I had no peace about, but I liked the salary. I literally cried on my first day of work because I knew that I was in disobedience. I *knew* that I wasn't supposed to be there. It wasn't some emotional thing, I just heard the Holy Spirit and straight up disobeyed.

Is that you right now? **Are you openly in disobedience but praying for God to bless your sin?** You could be in school right now, praying for God to bless your studies, but He told you to leave school, or you could be shacking up with some man to save money while you are praying for your purpose.

Maybe you are at a job that has already passed its expiration date; regardless of where you are, it's time to get back on track.

You cannot afford to be somewhere that you are not supposed to be. You have to make sure that you are in obedience to the Lord. Ultimately, I had to quit that job and get back in position because I found that disobedience hinders my prayers and my confidence. I won't go boldly before the Lord in prayer if I **secretly know that I am doing something that I am not supposed to do.**

So, what is keeping you from obeying the Lord? What are you afraid of? I worked in corporate America for nine years before I saw a ministry stage. The entire time I was there, I knew what God called me to do, yet still, day in and day out, I put my key card around my neck and went to work. I was present and active on my job because I truly wanted to work as unto the Lord. I knew that God wouldn't give me more if I was terribly unfaithful with little.

While I was at my job, I noticed that most of the employees came to me with their troubles. I didn't broadcast that I was a Christian, but over time, people would notice that I was a bit different in the office. I didn't curse, I didn't gossip about others, and when people asked me what my plans were for the weekend, those plans always included church. I simply worked that position as an assignment from the Lord. I wasn't aspiring to work there my whole life and I knew that God did not call me to be there for twenty years, but I was passing through for a season to work hard and as unto the Lord. Because of this, I saw fruit. I knew God was using me right where I was.

So what are you good at? I am good at Human Resources, Marketing, and connecting and gathering people to talk about Jesus. These things **come natural and are totally effortless for me.**

What comes natural to you that isn't normal or that doesn't come natural to others? Everyone is good at something. You may feel like you have no gifts or talents, but honey, God has called you to something specific. He has created you to solve a problem in this world and sadly, **some of us die out of position.** You stay at the wrong job for 40 years because you want their retirement package, while the entire time you are meditating and thinking about that thing God called you to do. You may be good at baking, but you don't feel like it's sufficient; all the while, God wants you to create a recipe book and start baking different things because that is what comes natural to you.

As you bake, you begin to post photos online of your creations and you let people know that you take orders. Soon, you figure out a way to ship your baked goods and a private investor tastes your cupcakes and absolutely falls in love with them. Then, the private investor writes you a check to open up your own bakery. You build the bakery and prior to opening it, you pray, and anoint that place with oil. You pray that it's a safe place for people to flock to in the midst of hard times. You pray that people come to Jesus in your bakery. You pray that people open up there and share their troubles, so that you may touch and agree. Then, you become the neighborhood bakery, and people fall in love with your baked goods. They drive 2-3 hours just for your cookies because they sense God's peace in that place. Some people that would never set foot in a church, visit your bakery, learn about Christ, and are then open to visiting your church. Isn't that amazing? All because of your steps of obedience!

Baking may not be your thing, but I want to share a few stories of interactions that I have had with women who were searching for their purpose in their passion.

"PLAYING IT SAFE"

A young lady was doing my friend's makeup while we were chatting about life, work, and family. I asked her what was she pursuing outside of makeup, and she mentioned that she was in school.

"School? That's awesome! What are you studying?"

She replied, "Nursing."

I asked, "Is there a reason that you're studying nursing? When you talk about worshipping Jesus through singing, I see your eyes light up. You're so passionate and excited. When you started to tell me about school, it seemed like your voice went dry. Any reason?"

"Well Heather, I have to pay the bills, don't I? Singing doesn't pay the bills."

"Well, last thing I heard, it's the Lord our Provider that takes care of those bills. You're in nursing school to make a few extra bucks a week, but you hate it. Not only are you wasting money using student loans, but you are putting more confidence in your flesh. You're wasting your time!"

"My mom was a nurse so it just makes sense. I need to find a way to support myself."

"Sis, I understand. Have you asked the Lord? "

"Well, not really. I figured that I would continue in school because I don't see how I can make money any other way."

"So, how are you paying for school?"

"Loans."

"You are taking loans to do something that you really don't want to do and something you pretty much plan on quitting once you are ready to start a family?"

"Yes."

Do you find yourself in this woman's shoes? If money was not a factor, she said she would be a worship singer. She has the most beautiful, sweet, and angelic voice. What if God wants to use her in worship? He may lead her to sing songs on Youtube, or share how important it is for worship leaders to set the atmosphere prior to the preacher sharing his message.

We need nurses; their job is very important, but she is taking someone's position that has been created and designed for nursing, someone who is *passionate* about nursing and believes that God called them to be there. **You are out of place because you weren't supposed to pursue that career.** God wanted her to lead worship and trust Him for wisdom on how He is going to provide. I wonder if she will be obedient to the Holy Father, or will she look up at 90 years old and regret that she never took that leap of faith? That she never even sat before Him and asked, *"Lord, what do you really want me to do?"*

Some of us need to go sit quietly before Him, and ask the Lord this question: **Not what I think I need to do, not what my parents think I need to do, not what society thinks I need to do, but what do *you* want me to do God? Then, act out on faith.**

"Nanny to Purpose Planter"

A friend of mine is a nanny and she's very passionate about children's learning and development. She gets excited about the school supply store and is always coming up with new ideas and ways to teach children. She creates the curriculum for the kids she homeschools, and thinks of different ways to make learning easier and more enjoyable for them.

I told her that she's really great at creating curriculum, and that it's truly a special and unique skill that not many people have. It's definitely not normal for me to go to sleep thinking about curriculum for 4-6 year olds. Matter of fact, the last thing I am thinking about is schoolwork!

After some encouragement, I suggested that she publish her unique curriculum and sell it; allowing her to create income from her passion! This young woman is naturally great with kids and her passion for children is evident in everything she does. She also desires to be a stay at home mom when she has children of her own, which continues to align perfectly with her passion. Although she may not see it as grand, God has graced her to help raise children to know Christ by teaching them His ways through school work. She is planting the very seeds that will one day bring that child to Christ! How *grand* is that?! With a change in perspective, she went from being a nanny to a purpose planter. "She plants, another waters, and then God makes that person grow (1 Corinthians 3:7)."

As she pursues making her passion a business one day, I will support her because we are home schooling our children. I will share her details with my friends, family, and others because I believe in *her* and the vision that God gave her!

"WIGS OF PURPOSE"

"Heather, I'm in grad school to get my psychology degree."

"Wait, why are you in grad school? I thought you had a passion for doing hair, making wigs, and sharing Christ with your clients?"

"I am passionate about it, but if I'm honest, my family consists of doctors, lawyers, and other 'high level' jobs. It's hard for me to be okay with saying I just do hair."

"You don't 'Just do hair,' it is a gift. It's a talent. It's something that God birthed inside of you for such a time as this! You are a hair engineer. A hair specialist. At what point did you believe the world's lies that said you have to be a lawyer, or a doctor to be successful? True success is when we are obedient to what the Lord told us to do. You were *created* to do hair and bring glory to God while doing it! Tell me about your hair business."

"Well, I want to make wigs for children or people that have cancer or those that deal with hair loss and cannot afford it. I like to do hair because when people sit in my chair, they pour out their lives and I end up counseling them. I truly believe that it is my ministry. I truly believe that it's what God has called me to do. It's just hard because everyone around me is doing 'big things' based on the world's perspective."

"The beautiful thing about you stepping out on faith with hair is that God paves the way for you. It may seem like you're taking a longer route, it may seem like nobody is supporting you, it may seem like you are purposeless, but one day, the very people that doubted you will congratulate you. It's not a thing of ego or pride, it's just the reality that they had to see you step out in faith, then see that you were successful through Christ. **God has a way of showing people much better than you can show them.** You just do what God tells you to do! Stop waiting for the approval of a bunch of people, and be led by His Spirit. This doesn't mean that all of a sudden things are going to be rosy, happy, or that you will make a ton of money, it just means that you take the daily steps of *obedience*. You will have rough days, you will have days where you don't understand, you will have hard moments, but being in the proper position for Him to use you is all that matters."

"The eyes of the LORD search the whole earth in order to strengthen those whose hearts are fully committed to him." – 2 Chronicles 16:9

God is searching the earth for someone who will live for Him! My friend left grad school and she has focused 100% of her time to doing hair, making wigs, healthy hair products, and other great things. I'm so proud of her! God birthed this natural talent in her, and she is walking in it. I called her recently to ask about her business, and she said it's so successful that she cannot keep up with it, and has hired people to accommodate the demand!

God is simply searching this earth for someone who will live for Him, and I ask you—*Is He finding you?* Can you believe that God is actually searching this earth looking to strengthen hearts that are fully committed to Him?

Are you fully committed to God? Even if they talk about you, if they don't agree with you, if you feel like a failure, if you don't feel good about yourself, are you still willing to refuse to back away from the calling he has put on your life? You know that He is doing a special work in you, and He will complete it until the day of Jesus Christ!

"Anyone who listens to my teaching and follows it is wise, like a person who builds a house on solid rock. Though the rain comes in torrents and the floodwaters rise and the winds beat against that house, it won't collapse because it is built on bedrock. But anyone who hears my teaching and doesn't obey it is foolish, like a person who builds a house on sand. When the rains and floods come and the winds beat against that house, it will collapse with a mighty crash." -Matthew 7:24-27

Are you letting the Lord pull up your foundation? To bring this a little closer to home, are you *okay with leaving the job that He is telling you to leave?* Are you okay with moving to another state even though you do not have "secure" plans? Are you okay with leaving that church that you've been at for 25 years, and you're only there because your mama is there? Are you okay with standing when you want to move?

This is part of the Lord developing us and changing us into His image. It's not pretty, you won't always understand, you will often ask for prayer, and you will at times feel lost and lonely, but this season is so beautiful because it is where you truly learn to trust in the Lord and cling to Him. If it were truly easy, everyone would do it.

Chapter 6:

Talent vs.

Purpose

My passion was birthed from my frustration with seeing women in a rut. I hated to see women that ran from the Lord, their calling, or seeing them covering up their gifts. I believe that the Lord puts talents in every single one of us, but **how do we know the difference between what we are good at, and what God has called us to do?**

It's simple. God *calls* us to do it, it brings fruit, others are blessed by it, and people come to know who He is through it. The proof is in the pudding. You may be good at a lot of things *naturally*, but see those talents manifest in your life differently than you would have imagined.

One of my passions is helping people. I simply love seeing people on fire for Jesus, and serving Him, but I did not see how it would relate to my purpose and keep me from working a typical office job. As I mentioned, I love marketing and I had so much fun working in that field; however, I have not been called to be a marketing director at a company. There is nothing wrong with working a 9-5, I just knew that I did not want to have one my whole life. I knew I wanted multiple businesses, and to work from home while raising our family. In ministry and with the Pinky Promise Movement, I am still able to use some of those marketing and HR skills for my own business, but I haven't been called to work in marketing as a 9-5 for this season. At the end of the day, we have all been called to do at least one thing. For me, it was a bracelet that turned into a worldwide ministry.

Colossians 3:17 tells us, *"And whatever you do or say, do it as a representative of the Lord Jesus, giving thanks through him to God the Father."* Whatever we do should bring glory to Him. You may be reading these words and at the same time, asking yourself if this, or that, could be your purpose. "God, have you called me to help people? What does that look like? Am I supposed to just leave my job? Should I go back to school?"

The point of this book is to ease that anxiety and remind you that it is **God alone that reveals purpose**. Not your flesh. Not your degree. Not your mindset. As believers, we put no confidence in our flesh (Philippians 3:3). Granted, it's ok to wonder, to ask the Lord, and to recognize what you're naturally good at, **but it's not ok to worry, fear, or become anxious about your purpose**. God will show you when He sees fit.

Isaiah 45:9 says, *"What sorrow awaits those who argue with their Creator. Does a clay pot argue with its maker? Does the clay dispute with the one who shapes it, saying, 'Stop, you're doing it wrong!' Does* the pot exclaim, 'How clumsy can you be?" We must trust in the Lord and trust that at the right time, He will show us. He isn't hiding in some corner, purposely trying to keep anything from us!

It's important that as you're seeking your purpose, that you are seeking the Lord. At times, we can become so focused and obsessed with our "specific" calling that maybe we do *nothing*. Maybe you don't serve, maybe you sit at home on a Friday night and complain that you have nothing to do, or maybe you complain about being a stay at home mother while feeling like you are bored with life. As believers, we must become faithful to God's general call to the kingdom. He has called us to be bold and courageous, to passionately love God and others, to be selfless, to help the poor, to pray for others, to forgive quickly and for you to live with a heart that is sensitive to His spirit. At times, we can get so stagnant in what God has called us to do, that we sit and wait for the calling we think we want for ourselves, instead of truly living for God until He reveals that to us.

Are you sitting around and waiting for God to show you? Instead, get up! Serve at your church! Help a single mother. Find a family that is super busy and go wash their clothes and help them cook dinner. Pray like never before every single day. Organize and clean up your house. Go workout. Grab a couple friends and start a bible study. What are you waiting for? Help the poor, feed the homeless!

"Well Heather, God didn't tell me to do that." Ok, did He tell you to go to the movies every Friday night with your friends? To the arcade? To the park with your kids? How is it that we only pull the "Hearing from God" card when it comes to being selfless? From sister to sister, me to you, I challenge you to step outside of yourself to help someone else in this season that you're in.

In pursuing Jesus to see what He's called you to do, I want you to remember this: **God prepares us overtime for what He has called us to do**. He may show you a small piece, before He reveals the entire pie. The story of Noah (Genesis 5:32-9:28) illustrates perfectly how when we righteously pursue God's will, He will give instructions for our purpose along the way:

When Noah was 500 years old, and the people on earth began to multiply, God saw that the life he created on earth had become dangerously enveloped in sin.

"And the Lord said, 'I will wipe this human race I have created from the face of the earth. Yes, and I will destroy every living thing—all the people, the large animals, the small animals that scurry along the ground, and even the birds of the sky. I am sorry I ever made them.' But Noah found favor with the Lord" - Genesis 6:7-8

Because Noah was the only righteous man on earth at the time, and "walked in close fellowship with God (Genesis 6:9)," God showed favor to him and his family. God spoke to Noah, giving him specific direction to build a boat because he was preparing a flood that would wipe out all that He had created. God told him the type of materials to use, the specific dimensions of the boat, and the exact number of animal pairs to bring on board in order to sustain life after the flood; all the while, encouraging Noah that he would, "Confirm his covenant to him (Genesis 6:18)."

When Noah was 600 years old, God did exactly what He promised, and covered the earth in a flood that lasted 150 days. Even after the flood was over, Noah and his family waited another eight months on the boat for the waters to recede, and for God to give them instruction to step back on earth. Once they were given permission to leave the boat, Noah immediately built an alter to the Lord and sacrificed animals as a burnt offering, that were specifically reserved for that purpose. The Lord was so pleased with Noah's obedience, that he promised to never again curse the earth because of the sins of humans, who had no choice in the sin they inherited. God blessed Noah and his sons for their obedience, and gave the final instruction to, "Be fruitful and multiply. Fill the earth (Genesis 9:1)."

Noah was a blameless man who had *close fellowship* with the Lord. **God doesn't hand out and fulfill purposes to people that aren't trying to have a close fellowship with Him.** Granted, everybody has an assignment on this earth, but it doesn't mean we will accomplish it, *especially if we choose to live outside of Him.* So, let's examine your life. Is it *lukewarm?* Why would God give you an ark to build if you refuse to spend time with Him, are rebellious in your spirit, carrying around an attitude, or if you think that everybody owes you something? Sis, I'm saying this in love, and with tears in my eyes because I want you to get this: **You have a part to play in your walk with the Lord.** You cannot ignore God your whole life and expect to be powerful for Him. God gave Noah instructions for 100 years, and Noah didn't even see a rain cloud. One hundred years, but God tells us to put our phones down to spend an hour with Him, and we can't do that because we are afraid we will miss out on comparing our life to someone else's highlight reel on social media. I simply cannot imagine how people must have looked at Noah during this time; how they must have mocked him while he was the only one on the *earth* that cared about living for God. I am confident that those around him laughed at his blind obedience to the Father.

God may be giving you instructions as well, but you must remain faithful and obedient even if you don't see the fruit of it yet. You may not see a rain cloud, but you are getting the exact measurements of what God wants you to do. I know it's hard. I know you don't understand, as I'm sure Noah felt the same, but just keep obeying Him in your today. As I mentioned before, I knew what God called me to do, but I didn't see an actual stage for many years. I encourage you to take your today, the tests that come with it, and face them head on with the help of the Holy Spirit. He will help you, lead you, and prepare you for the next step.

Chapter 7:

Mouth to

Heart Connection

As you are walking out this faith walk, I must ask, what are you saying? I sense that we are saying a whole lot, but there's no connection. We have no relationship with Jesus.

Can I be real with you? Confessing, "Today is going to be the day that you see your purpose, today is going to be your breakthrough," means nothing if you aren't connected to your power source. *Even* if you are connected to the Lord, there's a time and a season under the sun for everything, and when you *are* connected to God, you won't be running around proclaiming that you are getting "now favor, now money, or now purpose." Instead, you're crying out to the Lord for your sin. You're asking Him to break your heart for things that aren't like Him, you're asking Him to cleanse you of all unrighteousness. You see the difference? Instead of rushing ahead of the Lord, you trust His sweet timing because you know that your purpose will come to pass in due time.

Imagine if my phone died, but I kept telling you to call me. You would get pretty frustrated with me because, although I am telling you to call me, I cannot answer because my phone is not charged. I believe that the Lord is the same way with us. He constantly tries to reach us and speak to us, but we refuse to plug into Him. It's so simple to take your phone and plug it in, just as it's so easy for you to make that time to plug into the Lord. There's just something about plugging into Him, *then* speaking faith filled words. Those words will actually have power because they came from the source, the Lord!

Some of us are just going through the motions. We show up at church, we give, we volunteer and we do all of these "good works," but there's no connection—it becomes a routine. No wonder we get weary in well doing! God is saying that it's no longer enough to just go through the motions of belonging to Christ, instead a heart surgery needs to take place.

I've shared my story many times and I can honestly say that for years, I went to church, prayed, and served, yet I still ended up in the bed with my little boyfriend. "But, Heather, this doesn't apply to me because I am married." Well, that same rebellion from your single days can resurface in your marriage. It's a spirit that is looking to destroy your life, and to cause division and confusion. Nonetheless, I still disobeyed intentionally. Was I convicted? Yes. Emotional? Yes. Was there a heart change? No.

Isaiah 29:13-14 says, *"For they honor me with their lips but their hearts are far from me."* It's not enough to cry about your sin. Yes, crying is great because it shows that your heart is sensitive to sin, but it's time to repent of those things, and never return to the sin that once kept you bound.

I love the story of Paul's ministry in Ephesus:

"God gave Paul the power to perform unusual miracles. When handkerchiefs or aprons that had merely touched his skin were placed on sick people, they were healed of their diseases, and evil spirits were expelled. A group of Jews were traveling from town to town casting out evil spirits. They tried to use the name of the Lord Jesus in their incantation, saying, "I command you in the name of Jesus, whom Paul preaches, to come out!" Seven sons of Sceva, a leading priest, were doing this. But one time when they tried it, the evil spirit replied, "I know Jesus, and I know Paul, but who are you?" Then the man with the evil spirit leaped on them, overpowered them, and attacked them with such violence that they fled from the house, naked and battered."- Acts 19:11-16

Because the sons of Sceva were involved in witchcraft for profit, they were very impressed by

Paul's ability to drive out demons, but they weren't aware that Paul's power came from the Holy Spirit, which made him much more powerful than them.

Does the enemy know who you are? Are you a threat to his plans, or are you too busy serving in his kingdom? God's power is given to those that have a close relationship with Him, and cannot be duplicated. This is why you also don't need to be worried if someone "copies" your God-given idea! When you are connected to the Source, He breathes life into what He called you to do. He didn't anoint anyone else to bring that idea to fruition, He anointed you! How powerful!

Again, this is why you don't have to be jealous or concerned about what others are doing, or their opinions of you, because when you are connected to your power source— the Holy Spirit—you know that no human on this earth can take what God has for you. The sons of Sceva were calling on the name of Jesus without knowing Him personally! The power to heal, set people free, be delivered, walk in our purpose, and more, comes from Jesus Christ alone! God's power cannot be tapped into by reciting His name like a magic charm, or just because you created a vision board with the selfish things that you want on there.

"Whatever, Heather! I got my vision board, I'm going to write the vision and make it plain!" This is the problem, you wrote *your* vision and made it plain to your selfish desires, and then tried to tag God's name to it.

Many of us have taken Habakkuk 2:2 out of context. God told Habakkuk to write down the vision that He gave him for the evil, rebellious Babylons. What was written on those tablets weren't new cars, a new man, a new house or a degree—it was judgment. If you are planning on writing a vision and making it plain, I encourage you to write out judgment for your life if you are not obedient to the Lord, look at it everyday, and tell yourself that you must be intentional in your walk with Him. Some of us would do good to go home and burn our vision boards. I had to burn mine, not only physically, but mentally.

I wanted to host television shows, I wanted a certain car, I wanted this or that, but I didn't even ask the Father whether it was *His* will because I wanted what I wanted, all in the name of Jesus. You cannot have your cake and eat it too. You cannot be a disciple of Christ, and be a disciple for Satan at the same time. You have to choose which camp you are a part of.

During that time in my life, I only ran to God when things got hard.

Why is it that we don't seek Him as much when things seem to be going well, but when things fall apart, we seek Him to "fix" our issues? What if I ignored my husband, and only talked to him when I needed something? He would feel used. You don't like to feel used, so why do we do the same thing to God?

It's time to truly surrender every part of our lives to Jesus. When you really surrender to Him, you no longer chase jobs, money, or things that this world celebrates as success. You're so busy living for Him that He literally sets you up. Even as I say this, some of you are questioning these very words. Where is your faith? Why do you doubt Him? Why do we believe the lies of the world, but when God tells you that He is your Provider, you wonder, and flash back to times where you think you lacked, and question Him. You question God because you aren't connected to your power source.

I can visualize a boat sitting in the middle of the ocean. The engine has fallen off into the water and the boat is drifting with the current. This person speaks empty words and goes wherever the wind takes them. When God tells them to do something, they rush to seek the opinions of others and then they become confused between faith and doubt. They're double minded. James writes of the doubting person saying, "Like a wave of the sea, blown and tossed by the wind. That man should not think he will receive anything from the Lord; he is a double-minded man, unstable in all he does (James 1:6–8)." However, a boat that has its engine intact, and is connected to a source of power, can push against the wind and steer the boat to its assigned destination. This person looks to God for their answers, and has a clear path laid out for them.

A doubter is a double-minded person. Jesus had in mind such a person when He spoke of the one who tries to serve two masters (Matthew 6:24). As such, he is "unstable," which comes from the Greek word *dipsuchos* which literally means "double-souled" or "unsteady, wavering, in both his character and feelings." A double-minded person is restless and confused in his thoughts, his actions, and his behavior. This type of person is always in conflict with himself. They are constantly torn between the world and their desire to trust Holy Spirit by placing their confidence in Him. Likewise, the term "unstable" can be likened to a drunken man, unable to walk a straight line, swaying one way, then another. He has no defined direction and as a result doesn't get anywhere. Such a person is "unstable in all he does."

Stop stumbling. Let's no longer be double minded in our ways. Lets no longer compare our life to others. Lets no longer drift with the wind. Let's no longer speak empty words. Instead, lets lean on the Holy Spirit, stay connected to Him, and trust Him with all of our hearts.

Chapter 8:

Refusing to

Compare your

Purpose Pregnancy

One day, I took Logan to the park after buying him plenty of outdoor friendly toys. I was so excited because I felt I had covered all my bases from bubbles, a kite, and plenty of soccer balls and footballs. As Logan began to play with his toys, he looks over and sees another child with chalk and a bike. Logan comes to me and asks for chalk and his bike, which are at home, thirty minutes away.

"Logan, sweetheart, play with the toys that mommy bought you. You don't need chalk or your bike right now. You have toys."

"But mommy, I don't want to play with my toys, I want his toys."

I learned in that moment that even if Logan had chalk and his bike, he would eventually see someone else with a bigger, better, flashier toy, and, once again, not be satisfied with what he has. When we first get anything knew, it's super exciting! We love everything about it initially, but over time, the "honeymoon" phase of that job, the new car, or that new relationship is over. You get into an argument with your guy or somebody at work throws you under the bus, and all of a sudden that new thing is no longer exciting. The new car smell is gone, and now you start researching the next car you want to buy. You mention to your friends that you are "looking for a new job again." You compare your marriage to other people's marriages, and you begin to feel defeated.

We do the same thing in our walk with the Lord! We compare our gifts and talents, our possessions, and our looks, and then we work really hard to get what others have. Once we do have it, we find out that we still aren't satisfied. It is only God alone that can fill our voids and give us true contentment. It's a trick of the enemy to get our eyes constantly on what everybody else is doing, while ignoring what God is doing in our lives. What a silly distraction and a waste of time!

Have you ever thought: "Why does it seem like she always gets everything? The job, the purpose, the husband, and the favor?" Ever felt like God has singled you out, and left you alone during a season in your life? Instead of truly enjoying that season, you complain, murmur, and compare your life to everyone else's around you, while feeling like the Lord has forgotten about you. If you're in the midst of a pity party, you have taken the bait from the enemy!

The enemy is trying to get you to focus on yourself and tear apart everything that the Lord has built in you. I challenge you to examine where you have opened doors and welcomed the enemy into your life! A lot of married people wish they were single, and a lot of single people wish they were married. I've learned that it's a trick of Satan himself to get you to feel like the grass was greener in another season, but that grass is as green as your perspective.

Each season in your life carries its own frustrations, hard times, beautiful days, and growing pains. In trusting God for what He has called us to do, it's so important that we remember to stay focused on Him, in our lane, and on our faces before Him in prayer. If you have time to compare yourself to another person, then you, most likely, are no longer praying. When you sit before the Holy God in prayer, He gives you perspective on your life. He illuminates His will for you for that day, He reveals to you that His eyes are constantly on you, He shows you that the numbers of hairs on your head are counted, and He tugs on your heart to trust Him no matter what! Comparing your life to others just opens a new door in your heart for envy and jealousy to take over.

Remember that time you started as an entry level employee at that company? You were so excited just to get an interview. You prayed and fasted for that job, and you were so thankful that the Lord provided an open door. Six months later, all you can do is complain about your new boss and how you don't feel appreciated. You constantly show up late. You say, "Yes," to your supervisor, but your facial expressions reflect that you couldn't care less. You're insubordinate, rebellious on the inside, and there's nothing about your work ethic that screams "flexible." Work as unto the Lord? Oh, you mean work as unto yourself! You are about that paper. You are trying to get that money, and because of this, God will never be able to trust you with your purpose because you haven't been faithful with another person's vision.

Long before I dared to step into my purpose, I had to show myself faithful as an employee for someone else's company. I had to learn to be content as a receptionist for a year before I got a promotion. I felt so unimportant, but I knew that God placed me there for a reason. I would tell myself, "I'm working as a receptionist, but deep down I know that I have been called to preach the gospel of Jesus Christ and travel the world while proclaiming His name."

We have to learn to be content where the Lord places us or we will always be staring at everyone else's "toys," wondering when it will be our turn.Discontentment is a heart issue, and it's one that cannot be satisfied by material or physical things.Contentment is defined as, "The state of being mentally or emotionally satisfied with things as they are."

Now, the Bible has a great deal to say about contentment—being satisfied with what we have, who we are, and where we're going. Jesus said, "Therefore I tell you, do not worry about your life, what you will eat or drink; or about your body, what you will wear. Is not life more important than food, and the body more important than clothes (Matthew 6:25)?"

Jesus is telling us to be content with what we have. He has given us a direct command not to worry about the things of this world.

"For the pagans run after all these things, and your heavenly Father knows that you need them. But seek first his kingdom and his righteousness, and all these things will be given to you." - Matthew 6:32-33

From Jesus' words, we can conclude that being discontent is actually a sin, and it puts us in the same category as those who do not know God. **How scary is that reality?** All along we thought it was ok to be a little greedy here, a little unhappy with God's timing there, and God is saying, *"Unbelievers* seek after those things! I am your Father! I am with you! Stop coveting what you think you need to be satisfied! You need only Me!"

I love Paul because he was a man who suffered and went without the comforts of life more than most people could ever imagine (2 Corinthians 11:23-28). Yet, he knew the key to contentment:

"I know what it is to be in need, and I know what it is to have plenty. I have learned the secret of being content in any and every situation, whether well fed or hungry, whether living in plenty or in want. I can do everything through Him who gives me strength."
- Philippians 4:12-13

Paul continues to tell the Hebrews,

"Let your conduct be without covetousness; be content with such things as you have. For He Himself has said, 'I will never leave you nor forsake you.' So

we may boldly say: 'The Lord is my helper; I will not fear. What can man do to me?" - Hebrews 13:5-6

Yet people continue to seek after more of the things of this world, never satisfied with their portion in life. Thanks to Logan, we can see that we are born into sin, and with this mindset of constantly wanting more. As parents, we can either help or hinder this process. Are we seeking to give our children everything to satisfy them? Instead, be led by the Holy Spirit. No person can truly be satisfied by physical things.

Solomon, the wisest and richest man who ever lived, said, "*Whoever loves money never has money enough; whoever loves wealth is never satisfied with his income. This too is meaningless* (Ecclesiastes 5:10)."

"Be content with such things as you have," means, as believers, such should be our trust and confidence in God, that we should be satisfied with our condition regardless of our circumstances.

"For we know, assuredly, that if we are faithful God will cause all things to work together for our good."
- Romans 8:28

To worry means we do not trust God. The key to overcoming our discontentment and lack of faith is to find out who God really is, and how He has been faithful to supply the needs of His people in the past. As we continue to stay plugged into Him, He will remind us that our current portion is perfect for us, and He is all we need. The Lord warns us to guard our hearts because things grow there that could potentially distract us from what God is calling us to do and be.

Chapter 9:

The Garden of

your Heart

I'm excited about the garden I'm planting In our backyard. I have so many memories of planting fruits, vegetables, and herbs while I was growing up, and a lot of not so happy memories of pulling weeds! In preparation, I purchased a raised garden, some soil, worms, seeds and lots of gardening tools. Through the process, I've learned things like not planting corn next to green peppers. Corn needs its own area away from other vegetables because the roots and stalks can take over; same goes for zucchini, and cucumbers.

Recently, I was planting seeds in the garden and Logan was so excited—he wanted to plant as well. I had each portion of vegetables perfectly sectioned off. The kale in one place, spinach in another, red peppers over here, and the same with the Yukon and sweet potatoes. All separated perfectly. The one area left open was for the carrots, and Logan had the bag of carrot seeds. I gently dug an area for the carrots and opened the bag. I put a handful of seeds in Logan's hand, and told him to dump them in the hole. To my horror, my wonderful, independent, strong three year old whips the carrots and throws them *all* over the garden.

"LOGAN! What are you doing?! Logan, no sweetheart! The carrot seeds go right in this section, not anywhere else."

As I explained to him that the carrots will grow on top of the kale and red peppers, the Holy Spirit spoke to me: *"Heather, many people are the same way. Don't you know that when you listen to garbage television that sells you a vision, ungodly music, or the conversations of ungodly friends, that you will reap a harvest of what is being sown into your mind? Whether you like it or not, a harvest is coming."*

We don't believe what God tells us because our hearts are hardened; we're bored, and constantly falling asleep in prayer. You compare yourself to everyone else, and you're angry for what seems to be no reason! Seeds are constantly being planted in the garden of your heart! I didn't want those carrot seeds just thrown on my garden, so I had to get on my hands and knees and dig up every little seed that was misplaced or scattered about! Many of us need to do the same thing.

You need to get on your knees before the Father and pluck up those seeds that were planted in your heart. Those seeds of rejection that were planted when you were adopted. Those seeds of abandonment when your dad left your mother to be a single mom. Those seeds of inferiority that were planted when the guy you had a crush on at twelve years old, chose your friend over you. Those seeds that were planted when someone called you ugly, not enough, or whatever else. You may have forgotten about those seeds that were planted when you were a child, but guess what, those seeds have grown up and are producing a harvest in your life, in your relationships, on your job, and in your mindset.

Many times, we wonder, "Why do we think and act the way we do?" It's because of the harvest of the seeds that were planted. This is why the bible tells us that we must *renew* our minds.

"Don't copy the behavior and customs of this world, but let God transform you into a new person by changing the way you think. Then you will learn to know God's will for you, which is good and pleasing and perfect." - Romans 12:2

I believe that one of the greatest attacks from the enemy, Satan, is the attack on our mindset and our belief in the Father. He wants us to doubt Jesus and His precious blood. I'm reminded of Luke 1:45 where an angel had just appeared to Mary to tell her that she would be pregnant with Jesus. Elizabeth, Mary's relative, was overcome by the Holy Spirit:

"You are blessed because you believe that the Lord would do what He said He would do."

Many of us want the "blessing," but we don't want the "obedience." We want the car, the fine, 6'4, godly, praying man, amazing marriage, money or whatever else we think we need to be satisfied, but don't even intimately know the Lord! We don't spend time with Him, and when we do, we have this laundry list of things we want from Him. "Lord, gimmie this, and Lord, gimmie that. I need my breakthrough Jesus, I need my stuff, Lord!"

We have more faith in our jobs, our careers, families, and dating apps and sites, than we do in the Lord. We need these things to feel validated, as if Christ is not enough. To bring it back to the garden, we honestly have more faith in the tangible planting of a carrot seed, than we do in the Holy God. You trust that if you plant a seed, water it, and pull the weeds, that you will eventually see a vegetable. God promised that He planted purpose in us over 2,000 years ago, but we *still* doubt and question Him.

Shame on us! Help our hearts Holy Spirit! Give us a heart that will worship you! Give us a heart that will live for you! Give us a heart that is sensitive to your spirit! Give us a heart and a burning desire to spend time with you, and to sit at your feet! If you've been spending more time reading this book than on your face before the Holy Spirit, **you need to put it down and go pray.** How do you know what I'm saying is biblical? I am telling you that it is, and I'm backing it up with scripture, but I pray that the Holy Spirit confirms in your heart the words that you are reading.

I am also not trying to go to hell for anybody as I know that I will be judged on every word I write and speak; however, we have to know the Lord for ourselves! We have to lay out before Him and let Him show us the right way to go! He will show you when someone is a false teacher or prophet. He will tell you when to unfollow someone on social media because that person is lying to your spirit! We have to trust Him and practice hearing His voice.

When I first got saved, I did not know all the scriptures I know now. I just knew that I was lonely and dissatisfied with my life. But, guess what? God can work with an honest, and pure heart. Ask God to create in you a clean heart and to renew a right spirit within you (Psalm 51:10). Ask Him to deliver you from your past, your sin, and your ungodly ways! Many times, we feel like we don't know how to pray or what to say, but prayer is simply talking to the Father!

You can't keep planting seeds of negativity, gossip, slander, or fear in your garden and expect for joy to grow! It's time to start planting prayer, faith, hope, and peace. I now understand Philippians 4:8, which says, "*And now, dear brothers and sisters, one final thing. Fix your thoughts on what is true, and honorable, and right, and pure, and lovely, and admirable. Think about things that are excellent and worthy of praise.*"

God has a purpose for you! We have to stop comparing our gifts to others while wondering if God has forgotten about us! "God, why does it seem like so and so always gets everything? She's the leader of the ministry at church, she gets the man, the job, and the car. And, please explain to me how sister Susie just walked up in church and got saved, and she all of a sudden gets pursued by the 'most' saved, eligible bachelor in the church? She just got saved yesterday! I'm single, 28, and a virgin Jesus! When is it my time?!"

Ok, stop right there. **Where did the envy and jealousy come from?** It was planted somewhere. Go back to your garden and figure out what seeds were thrown over your kale, and pull it up from the roots. Were they planted while watching a show? While listening to music, or your favorite non-biblical motivation speaker? Was it planted when you were a child? Get on your knees and ask the Holy Spirit to break those ties with jealousy right now in the name of Jesus!

Have you ever envied people who God apparently singled out for special things? A cure for that jealousy is to rejoice with those individuals, and realize that God uses people in ways best suited to His purpose. You being jealous or talking badly about them won't prevent things from happening in their life. Remember Joseph's story? (Genesis 37) Joseph still became king even in the midst of his tests and trials. What about David? Even with Saul trying to kill him, He still did what God called Him to do. **You're actually tearing yourself down, cluttering up your own garden, and choking your vegetables from growing.**

I was so inspired when reading Luke 1:45 after Elizabeth was overcome with the Holy Spirit. Mary's response confirmed that what the angel said to her was filled with faith! After we receive a word, what are we saying? Are we full of faith? Or, do we sit on the idea, website, domain name, organization, or business while doubting what God called us to do. We post it on social media, asking for opinions as if we haven't already received approval from God. I can understand godly counsel, but all 1,452 of your pretend friends from elementary school don't need to have an opinion of your logo and business idea before you continue on with it. I loved Mary's faith. *She worshipped God.* She was excited and filled with faith. She didn't need to run around and ask for anybody's opinion.

How does one get to the point where they stop planting bad seeds? *Prayer.* What is your prayer life like? Have you learned to live without prayer? Many times, we get so busy running around, scheduling date nights, girl time, play dates, rehearsals, or whatever else that we never schedule time that is uninterrupted to sit before the Lord. We give the Lord the lousy lasts of our day, as we close our eyes and say some empty prayer. **God wants the best part of your day, not the worst.** You should pray when you're at your best, and when you can totally devote your undivided attention to the Lord.

"But when you pray, go away by yourself, shut the door behind you, and pray to your Father in private. Then your Father, who sees everything, will reward you." – Matthew 6:6

If you're at your best in the morning, wake up and pray before you start your day. Personally, I'm a morning person! I *need* to spend time with Jesus before my day gets started. He gets my life all the way together. At night? Not so much. That's definitely not the best part of my day, but it is the best time for my husband to pray and spend time with the Lord. If you have children, you may be struggling to find a time to pray and spend time with God. When they take a nap—"Oh wait Heather, I need to do the dishes, laundry, start on dinner, and shower." Honestly, I understand as a mama of two, but those things can wait.

Those duties are already dominating your day, and you're still wondering why you are always impatient and frustrated with your children. Your husband also gets the wrath of your empty spirit, while you constantly put pressure on him to satisfy your "needs," but those are really just voids that can only be filled by the Lord.

I have learned that we are passing down our bad habits and mindsets to our children, whether we believe it or not. You may preach one thing to your child, but they watch you yell, roll your eyes, and live in a discontent state, and guess what? "Bad company corrupts good behavior (1 Corinthians 15:33)." Yikes. Yes, I just used that scripture in relation to corrupting your children's behavior. I know it's a hard pill to swallow, but your babies are watching your relationship with Jesus and you are shaping their mindset.

Posting about God on social media, volunteering at church, or even working for Jesus doesn't replace spending intimate, uninterrupted time with the Lord. When my husband and I have a date day, we like to put our phones away, and look at each other's faces and talk. We used to take turns fussing with each other about always being on our phones, and not giving each other our full, undivided attention. How is it that we want other humans to pay attention to us 100%, **while we intentionally ignore God, scroll through twitter while in our prayer time, and sit there bored.**

Why are you bored?! You are sitting before the maker of the *heavens* and the *earth*! Do you know what that means? It means the One that created the entire universe, galaxies, stars, all of humanity, and who is literally the beginning and the end, desires and tugs on *your* heart. He wants a relationship with *you*. God alone placed the stars in the sky, and the very ocean obeys His commands! Rocks cry out and praise His name (Luke 19:40)!

Can you even fathom His greatness, and the fact that God desires a relationship with *you*? Now, tell me again why you are bored? You may feel like He is not there with you in your bathroom, prayer room, or corner, but I am assured of this truth: "'Can a man hide himself in hiding places so I do not see him?'" declares the LORD "'Do I not fill the heavens and the earth?' declares the LORD (Jeremiah 23:24)." The Lord is omnipresent! How reassuring is it to know that He will never leave us or forsake us, and that nothing can separate us from his love?

If you're struggling with what it looks like to spend time with Jesus, just begin by putting yourself in a position of worship. Whatever your posture of prayer, in whatever space or corner you're comfortable in— maybe with your favorite Gospel artists—pour out your praises to the Lord. The most important part is that you're pulling time aside to sit before Him. Starting with worship works well for me, and creates an atmosphere for me to begin praying in the Holy

Spirit, which is so important because it allows an intimate language with the Father that includes prayers that we can't even communicate in our native language. After prayer, I like to turn my music off, sit quietly, and let the Lord download into me what he would have me to know at that time.

It's here where He gives me instructions, perspective, and encourages me to trust Him in this fight. He reminds me that the battle is already won, and to continue to trust Him. This may be one of my favorite parts of my quiet time because the Creator of the Heavens and the Earth is talking to little ole me from Brooklyn, Michigan. What an honor! This is also the time that I like to vent to the Lord and tell Him what may be frustrating me.

He then takes me to different scriptures, and encourages me to keep trusting in Him. If my quiet time seems a bit silent that day, or the Lord isn't leading me to study anything in particular, then I will do a word study. Maybe that week I was struggling with submission, or trusting Him. Maybe I was struggling with feeling overwhelmed. From there, I study out the scriptures based on the index in the back of the bible. I also grab a concordance—a bible study tool that contains an alphabetical index of words in the bible and the main bible references to that word— to break down the scriptures. An internet search can also help when doing a word study, but don't depend on it too much because it's good to learn where things are in the bible through your own effort. Another useful tip is to study out each word or phrase in the scripture you're studying.

For example:

"Trust in the Lord with all of your heart and lean not to your own understanding. In all of your ways acknowledge Him and He will direct you."
– Proverbs 3:5-6

"Trust in the Lord"—Who do I trust? Am I really trusting in Jesus? My life should show who I trust.

"With all of my heart" –my heart, my ways, my will, my emotions, my feelings. Are they directed towards Christ or they directed towards someone or something else?

"Lean not to your own understanding"— So, there's a chance that I'm going to try to lean on what I've picked up over the years, or what I know to be true. There's going to be a fight to live for God.

What is my understanding? Where did I get it from? Is it biblical? How do I view being a wife, a

114

mother, a Christian? A friend? A CEO? Does my understanding line up with the Lord's understanding or not?

"In all of your ways acknowledge Him"—What are my ways? In how I treat others, love others, how I spend money, what I do with my time, how I raise our children, how I take care of my physical body and so many other things.

"He will direct you."— He will direct me. God is trying to direct me and lead me. He will direct me if I trust in Him, and if I don't lean on what I think I need to be satisfied. He will guide me if I acknowledge and include Him in all of my ways. God will speak to me and show me which way I am supposed to go, and what I am supposed to do. God has not forgotten about me, and He will never leave me or forsake me. My name is written on His hands and He knows the number of hairs on my head!

Do you see how full that scripture just became? There are times where I get stuck on one scripture for weeks. God's word is living, it's breathing! It's active, and the Holy Spirit will speak to you as you trust Him!

This is why you can't have some drive-by quiet time with the Lord! This is why you need to have time to set aside for Him. Not when you are doing a million other things. How can you take notes on what the Holy Spirit tells you if you are driving? I don't know about you, but I don't want to miss anything that the Lord is speaking to me about. I just want to please and serve Him. What if the Lord wants to instruct you to take a different route to work? I want my life to reflect and to look like His heart. How can I know His heart if I don't spend time with Him? Why do we expect God to share His secrets with us if we don't know Him? You wouldn't dare share your secrets with a stranger. **Many of us want the anointing and the fruit of the relationship with Jesus, without putting in any effort.**

If you truly want to hear His voice and want to position your heart to see the best fruit, then you have to start with getting to know Him and being intentional about sitting at His feet. Another way to insure that you are only planting good seeds is to obey God when He instructs you. When the Lord speaks, He expects to be heard and obeyed. Sometimes, we get so excited that the Lord spoke to us, that instead of obeying immediately, we sit on the vision, the idea, the blog, or the non profit for five or six years.

I truly believe that the Lord has sent you here to solve a problem during this generation. There is a reason that you weren't born in the 1400's or the

1500's. God has placed you here for such a time as this, but we allow fear to cloud our hearts. We just don't want to step out on what He says to us. Maybe it's people bondage, or maybe you just don't feel like you're "enough." Well sister, welcome to the club. You will never be enough outside of Christ. It is Jesus' death and resurrection that made us *enough*, and it's *through* Him we find value, worth and purpose.

So, what else has God been dealing with you about? Maybe it's cutting off a bad relationship, putting down the donut and eating healthy, cutting back on your spending and online shopping. Maybe it's working as unto the Lord at your job, or moving to another city. Whatever the case is, God is telling you these things for your good! Why do we think God sits in heaven, planning to make our lives miserable? Where did you get that from? What seed was planted along the way that has grown into a harvest of doubt?

"But Heather, I love this man. I want to marry him. We've been together for 4-5 years and I keep hoping that he is going to propose to me. I don't have total peace about him, but at the same time, I don't want to leave him."

"Does he know the Lord?"

"Well, umm... He goes to church with me here and there."

Church attendance doesn't equal a relationship, sis. Just because I walk into a wedding venue, doesn't mean that I am married. There are some practical steps that need to take place. Remember, whomever you choose to accept a ring from, will become the priest of your home. Let's break down what it means to be the head of your household. The seeds you let grow in your heart could reap the harvest of a unequally yoked relationship, and it is not worth it!

Help me understand how your boyfriend is going to wash you with the water of the word (Ephesians 5) if he doesn't know the word? What is he washing you with? Marry someone who can minister to your spirit, and stop focusing on men who can minister to your physical body. If you can say you're tired of being single, tired of waiting on the Lord, afraid of starting over, you love him, but deep down you know that he isn't right for you—let him go. He needs to find Jesus Christ and live for Him before He can meet you at the alter to say I do. I want you to read this note from a friend that married a man that she knew she wasn't supposed to marry:

"Heather, please remind these women of how important it is to trust God concerning a spouse. I didn't wait on the Lord in regards to my husband because I felt like I was getting old, and I already had four other children out of wedlock. At the time, my now husband would promise me all of these dreams of what our family would do once we got married. I believed him by faith, but while we were dating he proved to me that he wasn't the best at following through with what he said he was going to do. My husband is a great guy, but our marriage has suffered for years because I rushed and married a person that I truly knew was not ready. As Christians, we figured that as long as we had the Lord, we would figure out things later. I know that God was leading me to put the wedding on hold, but I ignored Him.

I feel like it's been test after test in our marriage and just now, ten years in, are we slowly starting to get along. At times, I feel like I lost myself and my life in the midst of getting evicted, barely having enough food, and not ever knowing the direction of our household. Now, I know that God is my Provider, but I also know that God warned me not to marry him. The invites were sent out, so even when my friends warned me, I refused to listen. Listen to the Holy Spirit. He will protect you from what you cannot see down the line.

I will never leave my marriage, but I wonder what things would have been like if I would have listened to the Lord. Fortunately, I have learned to be content after ten years of fighting. Nonetheless, this is my portion and I am owning it. I trust that the Lord will get glory from every decision that we make, now that we are wholeheartedly living for Him."

What are you rushing into? Maybe you are like this friend of mine who married someone that wasn't God's best. This is not the time to rush and leave your marriage "because you aren't happy," but instead, you get to develop even more with them.

Maybe it's a job that you rushed into. I can recall taking a job just because I wanted the salary, not because the Holy Spirit was leading me. I was miserable every single day at that position. Eventually, I left that job and three days later I had an interview for a position that carried our ministry in the early years. This isn't to encourage you to run and quit a job you hate, but instead, to not take the job that you don't have peace about in the first place.

Lastly, it's important that we are simply *willing* in our walk with the Lord. Many of us need to say, God, if it be THY will. Be it unto me Lord, as according to *your* will (Luke 1:45). Mary was willing to be persecuted, embarrassed, and shamed for being pregnant while not being married. God, if that means that I have to leave the church, the job, the ungodly boyfriend, or move to a new state, I will trust you. We have to remember that this is our *purpose* that is on the line. God is truly trying to lead and guide your life. We have to let Him.

Chapter 10:

Are You

Contaminated?

I believe that the Lord wants the garden of our heart to be clean so that the proper harvest can grow. Matthew 5:8 says, *"Blessed are those who have a pure heart, for they shall see God."*

As believers, we want our purpose, we want the godly relationship, we want the stuff, but we just don't want to wait on God to see what's on the other side of our obedience. Living for Jesus is going to cost you your whole life. God calls us to purity, whether single or married.

Purity is defined as, "Freedom from adulteration or contamination." Another definition describes purity as a lack of dirt, guilt, or evil thoughts.

Imagine two bottles of water that are filled halfway. One bottle represents a person with a clean heart and lifestyle, the other represents someone who doesn't guard their heart. As I pour dirt into the bottle of the person who doesn't guard their heart, I want you to imagine that this is what it looks like when you listen to ungodly music and TV, or hang out with ungodly friends and entertain unequally yoked relationships. That person's spirit man is dark, cloudy, and unclean. So, I ask you—what are you contaminated with? What are you pouring into your spirit?

Another definition of purity, is a lack of harmful substances. What you're watching, who you're hanging out with, and what you do is either helpful or harmful. At times, we give God deadlines because we aren't satisfied with our contaminated water. As you continue to pour dirt into your spirit you *attempt* to put pressure on God: "Lord, you're taking too long to bring me a man! Lord, you're taking too long to change my spouse! It's over! Lord, you're taking too long to bring this job! I'm going to just settle!" "Wait on you Jesus? Ok, I will wait for three months. Three. That's it. Not a second later because I want the manifestation of my prayers!"

I can recall a time where I gave the Lord a deadline. He was leading me to break up with my boyfriend, but I couldn't do it. I would tell Him that I would break things off next month, or the month after. I gave Him a deadline to what He told me to cut off immediately. Isn't it crazy how we justify these things in our head and think that we are being obedient to the Lord? I was not happy or satisfied because I continued to disobey the Lord and drink my contaminated water. Then, I began to pour out of my dirty cup in an attempt to preach one thing, but I was ruining my witness because I wasn't obeying God in small things.

How many people are drinking from your cup of contamination and are ending up sick because your heart is constantly polluted by the world? How can the Lord use you if you keep feeding yourself garbage? It can be difficult to sit and trust Him, especially when you just want to see things get better, but Matthew 6:25-34 reminds us to always be content:

"That is why I tell you not to worry about everyday life—whether you have enough food and drink, or enough clothes to wear. Isn't life more than food, and your body more than clothing? Look at the birds. They don't plant or harvest or store food in barns, for your heavenly Father feeds them. And aren't you far more valuable to him than they are? Can all your worries add a single moment to your life? And why worry about your clothing? Look at the lilies of the field and how they grow. They don't work or make their clothing, yet Solomon in all his glory was not dressed as beautifully as they are. And if God cares so wonderfully for wildflowers that are here today and thrown into the fire tomorrow, he will certainly care for you. Why do you have so little faith? So don't worry about these things, saying, 'What will we eat? What will we drink? What will we wear?' These things dominate the thoughts of

unbelievers, but your heavenly Father already knows all your needs. Seek the Kingdom of God above all else, and live righteously, and he will give you everything you need. So don't worry about tomorrow, for tomorrow will bring its own worries. Today's trouble is enough for today."

Why are you worried about these things while giving the Lord a deadline? You know what is beautiful about living for Jesus? As we repent of our sins, God pours out our dirty cups and *cleanses* us of all unrighteousness (1 John 1:9). We have to let Him pour *all* of us out! Our past, our dreams, our hopes, our entire life. Then, He begins to fill us up again through prayer and spending time with Him. He fills us up as we are led by Him to do the works of his kingdom. We have to let the Holy Spirit fill us up, over, and over again, as we pour out to bring glory to His name.

For years, I wanted my purpose, but I was contaminated! God couldn't send me anywhere because people would get sick off of my bad example. It's just not enough to sing the songs, but instead, we have to make sure that we are intentional about living the lyrics.

If the Lord placed me in ministry 10 years ago, I would have given Him a bad name; I wasn't ready. I had to stop chasing earthly things, and allow for His precious blood to really cleanse me.

When we really begin to let go of our life, it seems like things can get bad all of a sudden, and it doesn't feel good to get tested, but that is the Lord pruning your foundation and changing you into His image! He is making you more like Him! As you walk around as an empty bottle from being poured out by the Lord, you feel exposed, lonely at times, or just plain frustrated. You will lose friends because those people aren't going where God is taking you. Those friends are still living a contaminated lifestyle, and if you continue to surround yourself with them, they will pour out of their cup and contaminate you.

So, if you're feeling like you don't have the control over your life and things are a bit unsure, guess what? You're on the right track. Continue to live for Jesus and let Him show you the way to go! He will never lead you down the wrong path!

Pray this with me:

"Holy Spirit, I thank you for helping me to guard my heart against attacks. If there has been any contamination planted in my heart—I pray right now that you are cleansing me of all unrighteousness. I repent of all of my sins, known and unknown, and I declare that I will not allow for bad seeds to be planted in my heart anymore. I will not ruin my witness because I live what I preach! I walk by faith and not by sight! I will not look to the right, nor to the left, but straight ahead to the Word of God! I will not compare my life to others, I will guard my heart against covetousness, and I will remain sensitive to the Holy Spirit at all times. In Jesus name, Amen."

Chapter 11:

Birthing your

Purpose

My prayer at this point, is that you are starting to either see what the Lord is calling you to do, or you've gotten quiet enough before Him to hear specific instructions on your obedience.

I've learned that when you are pregnant, you get a lot of unsolicited advice from people, including their horror stories of their birthing process. Similarly, as you step out on faith in what the Lord has called you to do, you will have a lot of people with those same opinions, telling you what you need to do. As I mentioned before, wise counsel is great, but some of us are so hung up on the words of many that we aren't clinging to the words of the Only Living God. In order to be fully persuaded that the Lord has called you to do something, you must be confident and free from the opinions of others.

It's true, maybe you aren't typically transparent with people, maybe you are very guarded because you aren't used to opening up to others, maybe this, maybe that. Today, no matter what, we have to decide that we are going to be free from people's opinions. Remember, it is God alone that has birthed you, and told you what you've been called to do. You will never truly walk in God's plan for you if you are bound by the opinions of others! 1 Corinthians 9:19 tells us, *"Though I am free and belong to no* one, I have made myself a slave to everyone, to win as many as possible."

I am free from their opinions, I've developed beyond their ability to hurt me, and I have made myself a slave to serve and help others with the focus and intent of bringing as many people into the saving knowledge of Jesus Christ! *This* is our focus! While you're laboring, while you're going through the birthing pains of the tests and trials, while you're being persecuted for your faith, while you're being talked about, while you're feeling like you're not enough for your calling, remember:

"And I am certain that God, who began the good work within you, will continue his work until it is finally finished on the day when Christ Jesus returns."
- Philippians 1:6

He completes the work that He starts in you. Your purpose is *so* much bigger than you. It's not even *about* you! When I was trying to finish this book, I kept delaying it and the Lord woke me up one morning and said, *"Heather, the book needs to be completed tomorrow. It has to be finished. I want this book out because it's the proper time, and you are*

131

pushing the deadline. This book is not even about you, but who I am trying to reach."

Welp.

I only had a chapter or so to go, but I was taking my sweet time without any urgency. I have learned that delayed obedience is still disobedience. This book wasn't going to write itself. Your cookies won't bake themselves. Your law degree won't get handed to you. Your non-profit won't apply for itself. Your school won't start itself. You have a part to play in this journey. It is my prayer that you now have peace in knowing that He will show you His will in the proper time as you live for Him. He's not in heaven trying to keep things away from you, but He is also not going to reveal secrets to someone that He doesn't know.

If you've birthed that baby, or maybe you're now pregnant with that purpose and you're walking in it, I want to share a couple tips with you that I have learned along the way, walking in my own purpose:

1. Work hard, and as unto the Lord. Nobody is going to take care of your baby and business like

you will, and you can't expect others to care about it as much as you do. Pray for help and people that can join in and support you, but at the end of the day – it's your purpose, and your baby. Make sure all of your ground is covered.

2. Trust that God will bring the numbers. If you're hosting a conference, or starting a blog, or writing a book, you may feel like you don't have a market or that no one cares about what you have to say. In the book of Acts 2:47, it says "God added to their numbers daily," which tells me that it is God alone who brings the increase. Be faithful with little.

3. Make sure your paperwork is in order and that you are presenting a great product. Do the proper research on what it takes to make sure your baby is legit. God will give you the vision, but you still need to do the work of it. For example, as a part of having a business, I made sure that bank accounts were in the proper names, and that Pinky Promise was 501(c)3 approved. I also hired an accountant to make sure things were in order because I don't want to start a jail ministry due to unpaid taxes. :)

4.   Read a lot of books! There are so many small business books out there that can help with tips on running an efficient business. Do research on your expertise! As you stay in your lane, God can use other people that have been there, and done that, to help you out along the way.

5.   Be consistent. Just because your business has rough days, doesn't mean that you quit. Remember, God has graced you and *called* you to do what He has told you to do. Don't give up; the Holy Spirit is with you, helping you, and leading you along the way.

6.   Don't be afraid to ask for help. I have a team of people that help me, and I've learned that my purpose isn't a one-man show. God will send people to help you as you are obedient to his instruction.

7.   Surround yourself with strong believers and people that support your purpose baby. Don't hang out with gossipers that are satisfied with an average life, or sorta-kinda living for Jesus.

8.   Don't spend more time focusing on your business plan than you do in the presence of Holy

Spirit. We don't make idols out of our purpose. We serve Jesus, not our gifts and talents.

9. Don't hide your light. Sometimes, we try to camouflage our calling—which is to share Christ and bring Him glory. We don't deny Him to try to appeal to a certain audience. Be bold in your walk with Him. If you are going to be a Doctor, let people know that you serve the great Physician! If you are going to pursue law, be honest in your dealings. If you are going to preach, don't try to rip off churches by charging crazy amounts to come minister. Refuse to pimp the gospel.

10. Lastly, don't ever forget that it is God alone who gave you your gifts and talents. I know King Saul deeply regretted losing his anointing (1 Samuel 16). He lost favor with God because of his disobedience to His commands, and ended up committing suicide. At times, we can get so into our calling, and people can tell you that you're so great and wonderful, that if you aren't careful, it can go to your head. You may actually start to think that you're something special, but without Christ we are nothing. Pride will make you feel higher than you ought to be.

My prayer is that each and every one of you will have the boldness and the strength to step out and into what God has called you to do—totally unashamed and excited about living for Jesus, and doing His will. He is so faithful to us. Trust Him with your whole life and remember that one day, you will give an account for who you served on this earth, and what you did with the time that was given to you. Use it well.

God loves you like crazy.

Love always,
Heather Lindsey
www.heatherllindsey.com

Made in the USA
Charleston, SC
12 July 2016